PRE-POST-RACIAL AMERICA

SPIRITUAL STORIES FROM THE FRONT LINES

SANDHYA RANI JHA

CHALICE PRESS
ST. LOUIS, MISSOURI

Photo of Sandhya Rani Jha by Alain McLaughlin.

Print: 9780827244931 EPUB: 9780827244917 EPDF: 9780827244924

www.ChalicePress.com

"Our goal is to create a beloved community and this will require a qualitative change in our souls as well as a quantitative change in our lives."

—REV. DR. MARTIN LUTHER KING JR.

Acknowledgments

Special thanks to my incredibly gifted (and sensible) mother, Janette Jha, for helping create the questions at the end of each chapter as well as (alongside my equally gifted and sensible father Sunil Jha) having raised me with my faith and my interest in hearing multiple stories. Additional thanks to the many people of diverse backgrounds who helped me with the outline, chapter content, and fine-tuning my content; crowdsourcing is awesome! (Particular thanks to Riana Shaw Robinson, Derek Penwell, Yuki Schwartz, Ayanna Johnson, and Kat Hussein Lieu for feedback on large chunks of the draft manuscript.) Most of all, thanks to the inspiring people whose stories populate this book. I am grateful that you help me be a better person and make the world more and more the Beloved Community.

I would not see the world the way I do were it not for the Reconciliation Ministries of the Christian Church (Disciples of Christ) or Crossroads Antiracism Organizing & Training. Although most of my work is done in local community today, I thank God for both of them from the bottom of my heart.

Contents

Introduction

Complicating the Narrative— Stories of Living Race in America

"Power is the ability not just to tell the story of another person, but to make it the definitive story of that person. The Palestinian poet Mourid Barghouti writes that if you want to dispossess a people, the simplest way to do it is to tell their story and to start with 'secondly.' Start the story with the arrows of the Native Americans, and not with the arrival of the British, and you have an entirely different story. Start the story with the failure of the African state, and not with the colonial creation of the African state, and you have an entirely different story."

—Chimamanda Adichie,
"The Danger of the Single Story,"
TED Talk, October 7, 2009

My parents met at a college dance at Glasgow Tech in Scotland. I like to imagine their first dance was to a Beatles song, although I have no evidence to that effect. I just really love the Beatles, and they met in the fall of 1964.

My father was ten years old when India got its freedom and remembers taking turns with his classmates as night watch, sitting on the roof of the school in his village as they protected themselves against possible attacks in the wake of the bloody partition battles that broke out on August 17, 1947. My mother was born in post-war Glasgow, Scotland, and lived with ration coupons well into the 1950s. Interracial relationships were not much beloved when they met in 1964. My parents weren't political, and they didn't have a profound civil rights agenda. They just didn't care about the potential controversy; they liked each other. And eventually they loved each other.

So they weathered my mother being rejected by her family for loving a man of a different race and religion because they loved each other. And they weathered my father's family's deep ambivalence about my mother because they loved each other. (Today the family in India says he did even better than an Indian wife, because my mother has been so fiercely loyal to them.) And they didn't worry too much about the petition to evict them from the neighborhood when they first bought a home together, because they loved each other. And forty-five years since their wedding (fifty years since they met), they still love each other. And, better yet, they still like each other.

So my baseline narrative for race relations is a pretty inspiring one. But it is not uncomplicated.

It's complicated by my family's religious diversity: my father is Hindu and my mother and I are Christian. It's complicated by growing up on the outskirts of Akron, Ohio, where the five kids of color in my class of two hundred all strove to be as "standard American" as we were allowed to be, and since there were so few of us, we were pretty well accepted as long as we didn't claim any sort of difference. My school existence was complicated by hanging out with the Bengali Indian community on weekends, where the kids all ate pizza and watched football while the adults ate curry and talked politics. It's complicated by finding my voice as a South Asian in a suburban Chicago high school when I made friends with other South Asians while simultaneously being light-skinned enough to be mistaken for Greek, Latin@, Middle Eastern, Eastern European, and only very rarely identified as South Asian. And even that is complicated by the fact that for those who meet me in writing first bring a whole set of assumptions about who I am before we meet face-to-face. (This can be messy both in my consulting work and in online dating—you would not believe what some American men assume about South Asian women that meeting me in person cannot seem to disrupt.)

And yet my experience of race is very different than my parents'. My father, raised in a village where he was the same as everyone else, is sent to Toastmasters by his boss for not being a good public speaker, and when the head of Toastmasters says, "I don't know why you're here—you're a great public speaker," my father thinks, "Oh well—Toastmasters is fun!" instead of thinking, "That was about my accent, wasn't it?"

My mother hears a person at the luggage store where she works say, "I wish [all Indians] would go home," and she thinks it's a story worth telling over dinner but doesn't waste her time getting in the face of someone so ignorant in the moment, and doesn't give it more thought than that.

An Anglo friend of mine calls me an ABCD (American-Born Confused Desi[1]), and I kind of want to punch her—partly because I'm a little more radical and a little more antagonistic than my first-generation parents (although my mother's not exactly polite—subtlety is not a value imparted to the middle and working classes of Scotland—she just doesn't engage stupid). And partly I get upset because an Anglo person shouldn't be allowed to say that: I can make fun of my sister, but you can't. I reserve the right to mock my identity for real South Asians. (Although that hurts too.) But partly I get so mad because I grew up here, I grew up not being part of the norm, and I grew up—however much I tried to fight it—absorbing some of the very subtle messages that I was somehow less than. Being called an ABCD raises my own doubts about my racial identity.[2]

I also grew up only slowly realizing that race was shaping me at all, because it's become so darned slippery. So I'm not sure whether I'm allowed to be angry about something that may have been racial or may have had nothing to do with race at all. Did I get into that top seminary because they needed more diversity, even though my GRE scores weren't

---

[1]Desi is South Asian slang for a person from South Asia—India, Pakistan, Sri Lanka, Bangladesh, and Afghanistan.

[2]My friend Lynnette asked that I make sure to acknowledge the hurtful term "banana" used to describe Asians and Asian Americans who "act White." Similar terms for non-White racial and ethnic groups include oreo, twinkie and apple. They seem cute but can be hurtful whether used by people from other racial groups or our own.

the best, or was I a more impressive candidate than I think I am? Did I get almost no calls when I was in the search and call process to find a congregation to pastor because no one could pronounce my name, even though I was looking for the kind of church in very high supply and very low demand these days (dwindling urban congregation that can't afford a full-time minister), or was that just a coincidence? When I was a toddler and had just moved here, did the neighborhood kids push me in dog doo during hide and seek because they didn't like immigrants or because kids in Akron, Ohio, always pick on the little kid? Part of my anger is in not knowing.

We are one family with three different understandings of how race functions in our lives.

That is race in America: complicated and untidy. It is not knowable through a single story. Whenever we catch ourselves thinking about race as defined by our own experience, or the experience of that one friend we have of another race, we might be looking wrong at race. And yet so often, if we do not have multiple relationships with multiple people from a different race, we only have one narrative for people from that race. It's usually not a complicated narrative, and someone other than us usually constructed it.

As this book goes to print, we have received the grand jury decisions in both the deaths of Michael Brown and Eric Garner. In the media frenzy, both stories have been labeled complicated by some and very clear-cut by others. I have fairly strong opinions about these deaths, but regardless of people's opinions, the media illustrated Barghouti's point: "If you want to disinherit a people, tell their story for them, and start with 'secondly.'" The vast majority of narratives about those deaths have been from people outside the communities affected by them, and they do not by and large start with the context that created the grief and anger that poured into the streets. The absence of that voice certainly complicates the narrative, although not in a way that most of us are invited to notice.

And yet within these complicated narratives, I find glimpses of the realm of God here on earth, or what Martin

Luther King Jr. referred to as "The Beloved Community." For me, those glimpses seem to emerge because I have these conversations with people who are focused outside of themselves; they are instead focused on friends and family and neighbors, so that their struggles with injustice or with identity do not happen in a vacuum. At its best, that is what the life of faith gives us: the chance of becoming that Beloved Community.

I think it is no accident that we as Christians in America have as our primary text a book written primarily by a people who were defined by their religion but also their ethnic heritage. The Bible is saturated with stories of racial conflict, of overcoming, of surviving and of claiming power amidst defeat. These are stories that talk repeatedly about power imbalances and struggles. And they talk about God shining through in the places where men and women are willing to hear the stories of people from the margins, incorporating those stories into their lives in order to build communities of life and love.

The hardest part of examining race is to recognize that people's stories might actually contradict our own understanding of how things work. And at the same time, God might just shine through if we do not reject those stories but pay attention to the tension between someone else's experience and our own. If Mourid Barghouti is right that we wield human power over others when we tell their stories for them, then perhaps God's power emerges when we listen to and hold multiple stories and let ourselves be changed by them rather than seeking to control the narrative.

My purpose with this book is to share stories that help us look at issues of race in America through other lenses: stories of real people today, and stories of Scripture. Maybe these stories can help us reexamine our own stories, taking power away from those who seek to divide us and giving that power back to God. In the process, maybe we will celebrate that in the one race, the human race, we are made richly, gloriously, and uniquely in the image of God as part of one Beloved Community here on earth as it is in heaven.

1

The Civil Rights Movement Fifty Years Later

"The greatest movement for social justice our country has ever known is the civil rights movement and it was totally rooted in a love ethic."

—BELL HOOKS

"If not us, then who? If not now, then when?"

—JOHN E LEWIS

"I think that the thing that we learned back in the day of the civil rights movement is that you do have to keep on keeping on."

—CHARLAYNE HUNTER-GAULT

"Learn to do good;
seek justice,
correct oppression;
bring justice to the fatherless,
plead the widow's cause."

—ISAIAH 1:17 (ESV)

In my twenties, I worked in Washington, D.C. A friend of mine worked at a prominent civil rights organization that had been founded in the South at the height of the civil rights movement, in the 1950s and 60s. Its headquarters were now in Washington, D.C.

One day, in a pique of frustration, my friend said to the head of the organization, "Fred,[1] my generation is going to have to pry the civil rights movement from your generation's cold, dead hands, aren't we?"

"Yes," he responded without much humor; "yes, you will."

As I write this chapter, we are about to celebrate fifty years since the passage of the Voting Rights Act, which was functionally gutted by the Supreme Court last year, the year we celebrated the fiftieth anniversary of the March on Washington and Dr. King's famous "I Have a Dream" speech.

Many activists under the age of forty fear that the civil rights movement has stalled out and that those who witnessed the "I Have a Dream" speech don't know what to do with the *Dream Defenders,*[2] far less the *Dreamers.*[3] In the wake of Michael Brown's death on August 9, 2014, when young leaders of color emerged in Ferguson, Missouri (and the Dream Defenders took their skills honed at the state house in Florida after the George Zimmerman verdict and brought them to Missouri), the response to clergy participation in the protests was mixed, and one longtime civil rights pastor was booed when he asked protesters to donate to his church. Cornel West and a cadre of younger clergy were arrested on October 13 for peacefully protesting the lack of due process in relation to the officer who killed Michael Brown, and their actions were lifted up and appreciated, but leadership in

[1]Not his real name.

[2]The young people who staged a nonviolent takeover of the Florida state capitol in the weeks following the George Zimmerman verdict in the summer of 2013 and continue to organize in the wake of Michael Brown's murder in Ferguson.

[3]The undocumented college students who advocated for the Dream Act, protesting in Washington, D.C., and across the country, lying down in traffic in Atlanta, and crossing the U.S.-Mexico border and then trying to cross back in to bring attention to the unjust immigration laws that punish people brought into this country before the age of consent who are nonetheless subject to deportation laws that would send them to countries they are in no real way connected to.

the movement is from younger groups such as Hands Up United and #BlackLivesMatter, who do not see the previous generation standing with them or showing up for them.

And even as some Americans talk about two Americas or the New Jim Crow or a culture of anti-Blackness, we're also in an era where some people say we have reached the goal of being a "post-racial America," meaning they believe race as a category no longer matters, that we have achieved equality for everyone who tries hard enough. After all, we have a Black President, and things look very different than they did when people were being attacked by dogs and fire hoses and having crosses burned on their lawns.

As I write this chapter, however, our Black President has introduced the "My Brother's Keeper" initiative,[4] designed to address the fact that Black and Latino boys are far less likely to graduate from high school than their White or Asian counterparts (depending on which Asian subgroup you're considering) and are far more likely to be the victims of homicide. That doesn't sound post-racial to me. Nor does the fact that every twenty-eight hours a Black man is killed by police or vigilantes, according to Malcolm X Grassroots Movement. There has been debate about this statistic. The report writer's response to these criticisms (on theroot.com) is worth reading.[5]

Cornel West wrote a book in the mid-nineties called *Race Matters*.[6] He wrote it amidst attempts to repeal affirmative action programs and to completely rewrite food assistance and welfare programs, debates saturated with racial overtones, except that when people of color said race played a role in these conversations, they were accused of "playing the race card."

Twenty years later I think about Dr. West's book and wonder, Does the United States still think race matters? Fifty years after the passage of the Voting Rights Act (and the Immigration Rights Act that allowed my family to come

---

[4]More information available at: http://www.whitehouse.gov/my-brothers-keeper.

[5]See http://www.theroot.com/articles/culture/2014/12/_every28hours_author_responds_to_the_fact_checkers.html.

[6]Cornel West, *Race Matters* (New York: Vintage Books, 1994).

to the United States in the late 1970s, and many other civil rights bills), what does civil rights look like?

I'll be looking at race issues from many different perspectives throughout this book, but when we talk about race in the United States, I would guess that about 80 percent of the time, we're talking about Black-White issues. Sometimes we're talking about immigration, but usually we treat that as a completely different issue than race (even though it's a very racialized conversation). And when we're talking about race, we're rarely talking about Asian, Latin@, Native American, or any other groups. And, frustrated as I can get with being left out of the dialogue, it's not without reason.

There is nothing I can write about the legacy of slavery that can compare to what has already been written. Our modern day understandings of race were formed, I believe, because White indentured servants and Black slaves in the 1600s American colonies came together in rebellion against their ill treatment by wealthy White landowners. In the wake of the rebellion, the pseudo-science of race began to emerge, claiming White intellectual superiority and justifying the rapid expansion of chattel slavery while the role of the less cost-effective indentured servants (usually White) diminished and disappeared. The power of poor Black and White people united was too great a threat to those with power.

Sometimes people say, "Black people need to get over it; slavery was hundreds of years ago." My mother recently said on this subject, "Yes, but a man being arrested in the South for no reason and being beaten to death by a crowd on the Florida border solely for being Black wasn't hundreds of years ago; it was sixty. The last lynching wasn't hundreds of years ago; it was in the late 1960s. People not being allowed to vote wasn't hundreds of years ago; it was fifty years ago. A Black young man being shot for wearing a hoodie, or playing rap music in his car, or for standing on a corner a week before his high school graduation, wasn't hundreds of years ago; it was three years and two years and one year ago." And as a friend of mine said in the wake of the non-indictment of the officer in the choke-hold death of Eric Garner, "I would tell you what modern-day lynching looks like, but I. Can't. Breathe," quoting Garner's last words caught on tape before he died.

And at the same time, the landscape has certainly changed. I sat down with three different clergy colleagues from three different generations to learn from them what civil rights means today and how that has changed over the years. Rev. Phil Lawson (brother of Rev. James Lawson, prominent leader of the Student Nonviolent Coordinating Committee during the height of the civil rights movement) is just past eighty years old and at the height of his movement building work. Rev. Clarence Johnson is about sixty-five years old, just old enough to have participated in his pre-teen years in the March on Washington. Rev. Andrea Davidson is about forty years old, and she was born well after the March on Washington happened.

I wanted to talk to all three of them, because I have worked with them on issues of equality and civil rights today in the Bay Area, and because they are all African American clergy in predominantly White denominations, although they pastor or have pastored predominantly Black congregations. And, for the sake of transparency on my part, I also talked with them because they all engage in civil rights work for the Black community and also in solidarity with people of other communities, whether it be advocating immigration rights or gay rights, fasting with displaced workers, sleeping outside city hall with homeless people, or advocating in Sacramento for jobs and education equality. I wanted to know how these allies of mine understand the arc of the civil rights movement over the past fifty years (or more).

Rev. Lawson (then just "Phil") grew up in northeastern Ohio, not far from where I grew up. However, the region he grew up in looked a lot different than mine. "I wasn't *inspired* to participate in the civil rights movement," he clarifies. "I was propelled. I was pushed. I was driven—because I was born a Black man in northeast Ohio in 1932, at a time of segregation, a second-class citizen, constantly under threat, in an era when upwards of 100 black men and women were lynched every week across the United States. I was not even safe in my own United Methodist Church, which was segregated in terms of Blacks and Whites." By the time he was in his early teens, he was involved in the civil rights movement, although he is quick to point out that civil rights was only a step on the way to the healing of the soul of America, and "we were not focused on civil rights; we were focused on saving our nation, with the emphasis on *our,* like when you pray, you pray *our* Father."

I love Rev. Phil's ability to be fully and deeply committed to nonviolence ("I had to as a matter of living my faith; if you follow Jesus, you follow the path of love and nonviolence; there's no other way to read it") while standing beside people who disagree with him. In 1967, when several student ministers came to work with him in Kansas City, he sent them into the streets to develop relationships with the young men who had rioted and burned down part of the city. They learned that the young men wanted to start a chapter of the Black Panthers: "I didn't agree with the violence of the Black Panthers, but I supported these young men." His Methodist church helped the young men start a chapter in Kansas City, and because of the depth of their relationship with one another, he was able to negotiate between the police department and the Panthers[7] so that their chapter was the only one that did not to end up in a stand-off with the police.

While Rev. Lawson was coming into leadership, Rev. Johnson was watching his brother pastor East Percy Street Christian Church, part of the Disciples of Christ denomination.[8] He was twelve in 1963 when his brother hosted a

[7]The police and Panthers agreed that whenever the police believed illegal activity was happening in one of the Panthers' three houses, the Panthers would agree to let the house be inspected by the chief of police and Rev. Lawson. This avoided random questionable raids and the escalation that could result (and did result in other cities like Oakland and Chicago).

[8]As proud as we Disciples are of our Christian unity, it is interesting to note that the predominantly Black East Percy Street Christian Church was originally known as First Christian Church of Greenwood, Mississippi, until the predominantly White First Christian Church of Greenwood, Mississippi, across the river sued them for using the same name, although it may well have been the Black church that had the name first.

group of civil rights leaders who inspired and energized him. Also at the age of twelve, he was arrested with a group of people for registering voters in his hometown. I recently delighted my twelve-year-old niece when I told her this story, because he said he was arrested at 10 a.m., and his mother and a leader from the denominational office came to release him at 6 p.m. that same day; his understated comment was, "I've never been so glad to see two people in all my life." (A twelve-year-old can imagine how much you'd want to see your mother at the end of a whole day in jail, even if she doesn't totally understand why a twelve-year-old would get sent to jail for registering people to vote. Come to think of it, neither can a thirty-eight-year-old.) Clarence was also at the March on Washington that summer, and he remembers seeing celebrities such as Harry Belafonte and Mahalia Jackson walk by, although he doesn't remember Dr. King's speech, since he was hanging out by the reflecting pool with friends he had made that day from North Carolina.

By the summer of 1965, his mother had sent him to Youngstown, Ohio, because she thought it was too dangerous for a young Black man walking the streets of Greenwood wearing civil rights buttons as the situation got increasingly violent. However, the movement was too deep in his bones for that to be the end of the story. Rev. Johnson went on to organize the Disciples of Christ's Black Ministers Retreat and many other programs for Black Disciples churches before coming to the Bay area to do union organizing, advocate against apartheid in South Africa, and now pastor Mills Grove Christian Church in east Oakland, where he is recognized as a prominent civil rights leader in the city. He may have had more fun hanging out at the reflecting pool at the March on Washington, but his continued work standing with and praying with poorly treated workers and seniors facing safety issues hearkens back to the official theme of that march: The March for Jobs and Freedom.

Rev. Davidson grew up at about the same time I did, when she was known as Andrea in a working class neighborhood of Long Island that was mostly Black, but also Jewish and Italian. Andrea didn't grow up in a family or church or community that engaged in issues of civil rights all that deeply in the 1980s. They were incredibly charitable, and they were deeply faithful (in fact, Andrea grew up a preacher's kid at a Baptist church that might be classified as part of the Pentecostal or holiness movement), but they were definitely not political or really oriented towards any sort of focus on systems of justice. It is impossible to grow up Black in America and be unaware of discrimination and different treatment of Blacks compared to Whites. Nonetheless, the message Andrea received growing up was to focus on being her best spiritual self at all times; "fighting the system" just wasn't part of the narrative at home or school or church.

It may have been the era or it may have been the church (although many Americans assume that all Black churches are politically engaged and always have been, which simply isn't true as a universal statement), but Andrea's journey to become engaged in civil rights as a United Methodist minister was a journey of gradual discovery and study on her own, through a Black studies minor in college and through the realization that her profitable corporate job wasn't bringing her fulfillment. So the Rev. Davidson we encounter today is one whose spirituality has been shaped by a loving faith community, learning to integrate civil rights into that spirituality outside of her family and church. I know her through her work as a key leader with Oakland Community Organizations, an interfaith advocacy group working on ending violence and increasing education equity in the city of Oakland.

I've always thought I had a pretty good understanding of the civil rights movement. I studied it extensively, I debated it with my friends, I have personal relationships with both Black and White leaders who were involved on the front lines of the struggle in the South, in Chicago, in Boston, and in Oakland. I know the tensions within the movement as well as the pressures from outside of it. I know the role of the U.S. government's counterintelligence agents (ominously referred to as COINTELPRO) in undermining the Black Panthers.

But then last year I read *The Warmth of Other Suns* by Isabella Wilkerson about the Great Migration from the South to the North after the Civil War. It breathed life into what it meant to grow up Black in the South after slavery and before the civil rights movement. Being Black then meant people would steal from you (sharecropping), blame you for crimes you did not commit and murder you, or kill you for looking at them in a way they didn't like, all without any legal recourse. In a recent article on the website *The Daily Kos*, a man talked about coming home from college in the 1980s, radicalized by his Black studies courses and telling his father how Stokely Carmichael, Huey Newton, and Malcolm X had it right, and how Martin Luther King was an accommodator. "My father told me with a sort of cold fury, *'Dr. King ended the terror of living in the south.'*"[9]

A critical first step in building the Beloved Community is making sure no one has to be in perpetual fear for their lives. I think that we sometimes overlook this step because we take it for granted, although recent attention to the many deaths of unarmed Black men and boys such as John Crawford, Tamir Rice, Michael Brown, and Eric Garner make it harder to take for granted, that there are communities that do have to teach their children how to avoid being a target for unsolicited violence, knowing that might not be enough to protect them. And while we continue to address that first step, maybe the next step is making sure everyone has some reason to hope for the future.

In many ways, across generations, all three of the leaders I'm lifting up in this chapter are doing exactly that. All three are deeply involved with the modern day civil rights (and Beloved Community) issue of mass incarceration.

If you haven't read Michelle Alexander's *The New Jim Crow*,[10] you need to put this book down and pick that one up. What Upton Sinclair's book *The Jungle* did for health standards (and was supposed to do for working conditions

---

[9]Hamden Rice, "Most of you have no idea what Martin Luther King actually did," *The Daily Kos*, August 29, 2011, http://www.dailykos.com/story/2011/08/29/1011562/-Most-of-you-have-no-idea-what-Martin-Luther-King-actually-did#.

[10]Michelle Alexander, *The New Jim Crow* (2010; repr., New York: The New Press, 2012).

in meat packing plants), what Rachel Carson's *Silent Spring* did for the environmental movement and Betty Friedan's *The Feminine Mystique* did for feminism, *The New Jim Crow* is doing for the modern civil rights movement. It is telling a story that many of us in urban communities already know, but it is adding facts to the stories, letting us know we're not crazy and letting us know things might actually be more serious than we thought they were. The book is about the mass incarceration of Black people in America, not simply because they commit more crimes than other people or because poor people are arrested at greater rates than rich people, but because the judicial system has an inherent bias against Black people. (I totally understand if you don't believe me making that statement without any facts; read the book.)

In addition to mass incarceration, Rev. Johnson has established a summer Algebra Institute modeled on a program started by civil rights leader Robert Moses to address the achievement gap particularly between Black (and Latin@) children and White children in schools—studies have shown a difference in the way Black children are disciplined (more harshly) and attended to (less) in the earliest years of school in comparison to White children, even in the same classroom by the same teacher.[11] Some Black leaders are stepping up and filling that gap themselves through programs such as the Algebra Institute.

Rev. Davidson had her congregation study *The New Jim Crow* and is engaged in advocacy around more just sentencing laws in California, but she sees another element of the civil rights movement today. Rev. Davidson pastors a middle class Black congregation in a poor (mostly) Black neighborhood. Congregants drive in for worship and programs but do not live in the neighborhood. When I asked Andrea what the civil rights movement looks like today, in addition to the issue of mass incarceration, she said, "Connecting my congregation with this community." Building up solidarity across classes

[11]For more on this issue, read, "My son has been suspended five times. He's 3," Tunette Powell, *The Washington Post*, July 24, 2014: http://www.washingtonpost.com/posteverything/wp/2014/07/24/my-son-has-been-suspended-five-times-hes-3/.

is a central element of building the Beloved Community, especially when those who have made it might not always want to be reminded that they are connected to those who haven't.

Rev. Lawson works to lift up this issue and the issue of restorative justice (with space for remorse and forgiveness and rehabilitation) in partnership with a man recently released from prison after more than fifteen years. Along with the issue of mass incarceration, Rev. Lawson advocates for pretty much every justice issue imaginable, from immigration to gay and lesbian rights to economic justice. He also encourages young leaders to shape today's movement for justice in their own fashion—one of his critiques of the Occupy movement was that many activists of his generation and mine, shaped by the twentieth century, would not support anything that looked different than what we were comfortable with. If my friend had asked him about prying the civil rights movement out of his cold, dead hands, Rev. Lawson would say, "No, here: make it your own. Just let me work on it alongside you." In fact, a year before tanks rolled through Ferguson, Missouri, Rev. Lawson worked with me and an interracial, intergenerational, and interfaith group working to stop "Urban Shield," a police militarization program in our community. It involved Israeli military training our police in counterinsurgency tactics, and weapons like drones and tanks were available for low-cost purchase by local police departments.

Throughout this book, I look at each story in relationship to a specific story from the Bible. With this chapter, however, I find myself thinking instead about "biblical hermeneutics": *how our location in this moment in history in this country and with our own lived experiences shapes the way we read the Bible.* Each of the pastors mentioned in this chapter entered the world at a different time and in a different state, impacted by different manifestations of racism in their communities. They were also shaped by different gender and educational opportunities. As a result they each read (and experience) the civil rights movement of the past and the present differently.

Jesus, Peter, and Paul experienced God in very different ways, shaped by their lived experiences, their genealogies, and the communities they grew up in. As a result, all three of them envisioned the movement differently. I understand the impulse to say, "Well, I'm following it the way Jesus meant it to be done." I've said it myself, and my denomination was founded on the same argument. But Paul and, to some degree, Peter heavily mediated Christianity as we practice it today. And both of them practiced Christianity differently than Jesus, at least as the gospels lay out his teachings. Of course, they acted differently because they brought different hermeneutical lenses to their practices. Peter was a thoroughly Judean Jewish fisherman before joining Jesus' followers, and Paul a thoroughly Hellenized Jew who knew how the mercantile world of all sorts of non-Jews worked.

When we read the Bible, we do not read it through the eyes of a first-century Judean. As a result, we miss some of the jokes. Certain names do not evoke terror in our hearts as they would have for the founders of our faith. We are not shaped by the same relationship with God or the same relationship to the Hebrew Bible and its laws. We don't know what it means for our government to humiliate our religion and to view us as a unique threat because we believe God is more powerful than the head of our government.

When we read the civil rights movement, we each read it through our own hermeneutical lens and the same thing happens: we miss some of the jokes. Certain names do not evoke terror in our hearts as they would have for the people who risked and lost their lives before and during the movement.

Civil rights leaders must feel defeated when they have to fight the same battles today that they fought fifty years ago, and have been met with so much apathy by the wider U.S. public, who do not necessarily know or care much about education disparities or mass incarceration. It must feel frustrating to work in communities that struggle with the same issues as fifty years ago, except additionally ravaged by the crack epidemic of the 1980s and the war on drugs that has locked up far more Black people than White people for the same crimes, then sent them back to their communities without a chance at most jobs. (Think about the last job application you filled out; it probably had a box that said, "Check this box if you have ever served time in prison." Ask yourself, How many people who checked off that box do you think got called back for an interview?) For Andrea, it sometimes feels as if the civil rights movement disappeared during the 1980s, overwhelmed by the war on drugs or by respectability politics.[12] It can feel for many people in Rev. Davidson's generation that we're starting the movement building work from scratch.

Rev. Davidson and I have a lot in common as people from the same generation, neither of us yet born when the March on Washington or the assassination of Dr. King occurred, both women of color shaped by the liberation theology we learned in seminary instead of from the pulpit growing up (and find ourselves minorities in terms of pastors who preach liberation theology from the pulpit today), both of us women in a church that doesn't always know what to do with female clergy and even less what to do with female clergy of color (within our racial/ethnic communities and within our neighborhoods and within our mostly White denominations). When I asked Andrea what shoulders she stood on from the civil rights movement, she paused for a long time, and repeated the question: "Whose shoulders do I stand on? The shoulders of the women in the movement; the shoulders of women who did so much of the work and whose names we were never taught."

I asked Rev. Lawson what he thinks about the notion that we are a post-racial society. He laughed for a really long time, and then said, still laughing, "It's garbage. A characteristic of empire is its ability to co-opt everybody. The Beloved Community is not about good feelings. It is not about whether 'you like me.' It is about demographics. It's about evaluating who's at the bottom of the ladder, and who is not at the table. Slavery was never an issue of, 'Do you like me?' It was an issue of a system that some people are worth more than others. And that has not changed."

---

[12]Respectability politics is a description of the phenomenon within a movement such as the civil rights movement, which, upon experiencing some success for some members of the movement, creates cultural standards that separate those who have succeeded and adhere to those cultural standards from those who haven't succeeded and don't adhere to those cultural standards.

When I asked Rev. Johnson how he handles the fact that voter suppression is expanding rapidly at the same time the Voting Rights Act has been repealed, he responded as only the heartiest activist and the most faithful pastor could: "But we know we can prevail because we've been here before and we know the victory is already written."

Phil, Clarence, and Andrea approach the civil rights movement of today very differently; their lived experiences are different and the way they articulate their commitments is different. Their hermeneutics are different. When I think of Rev. Lawson, I can almost hear his frustration when I don't always remember that every act of justice is connected to all of the rest of them; it is not possible to draw a circle too wide for him. When I think of Rev. Johnson, I think of someone whose constant and consistent regard for others unconsciously requires you to approach him with the same regard and respect. I have never heard him say a disparaging word about another human being, even while he never shies from proclaiming his values. Rev. Davidson is bold and strong in her public commitments to justice, someone I can as easily picture with a bullhorn in front of city hall as I can see standing in the pulpit in a robe.

It is a real honor to work alongside clergy who are building (or rebuilding, or continuing to build) the Beloved Community today. Their voices are not necessarily one. That is important to note because we often make a mistake of shying away from acknowledging multiple perspectives from communities of color, because issues related to race are already so complicated. But the Beloved Community is strongest when all voices are heard and when we do not impose some sort of uniformity on various groups out of fear of disagreement.

And that's part of the point of this book. If we don't find a way to listen to one another's stories across difference, recognizing that even within racial/ethnic groups we have a broad array of experiences that we need to honor, we'll keep rebuilding the foundations of the Beloved Community over and over again. Why? Because those of us building it will get so frustrated at being ignored or villainized or homogenized that we'll take a sledgehammer to the unstable foundations and have to start from scratch. It's happened before. And lack of concern about one another's narratives has led to neglect of the load bearing walls.

I want to acknowledge, and I know all of the other clergy in this chapter would want me to acknowledge, two other people I get to work with. Neither of them is an ordained minister, and I've never heard either one of them describe their work as "civil rights work." Rayna and John grew up in Oakland at the height of the crack epidemic's tearing apart of the city. I've stood with both of them as they testified in front of the Port Commission about creating fair wage local hire jobs that give a second chance to people who are formerly incarcerated. Rayna, in her mid-twenties, has testified, baby on her hip, about losing her mother to violence that could have been prevented if our city had any opportunities for young people in the community. (Nothing stops a bullet like a job, says Father Greg Boyle of Los Angeles.) John, nearing 40 like Andrea and me, shares his struggles to find work that will support his family since the only jobs available to people who have been in prison are minimum wage jobs. In California, to afford rent for a family of four, a person paid the state minimum wage has to work 120 hours a week. They are fighting for jobs with dignity and an end to violence in their neighborhoods.[13] They are my community's Dream Defenders or Hands Up United making a better world for their babies in the face of a lifetime of injustice. The March on Washington was called the March for Jobs and Freedom, and it seems clear that Rayna and John are part of that legacy, demanding that my generation and older join them in the struggle or get out of the way. Their hermeneutic is one of the urgency of the present moment, and I know that Phil, Clarence, and Andrea will not force them to pry the civil rights movement out of their cold, dead hands.

---

[13]John recently got hired to mentor Oakland youth with a local non-profit. When Oakland passed a 12.25 minimum wage bill that John had been campaigning for, his son asked, "will we have more money now?" and John laughed and said, "Your father's not working at Burger King now. We get to live on a LITTLE more than even 12.25 an hour."

I believe the civil rights movement in America needs to be spiritually grounded and also needs to create a space where the very diverse communities of this nation listen deeply to each other. For White people, this *might* mean letting go of defensiveness, guilt, or maybe even a sense that the narratives of people of color have little to do with them. For people of color who rarely get our stories heard, it might mean pausing, catching a breath, and trying to hear the stories of other people of color and from White people that help us see one another in a new light and allow us to go deeper with one another, to name deep hurts and possibly create real healing. This book won't focus exclusively or even primarily on one particular race or ethnicity, but it was really important to me to begin by listening to some of my African American brothers and sisters. The spoken and unspoken narrative about race in America is shaped deeply by the nation's legacy and laws and practice in relationship to Black people, and I don't know how to do the work of Beloved Community without starting my journey of listening here.

CHAPTER QUESTIONS

1. Discuss whether the civil rights movement was successful—by your definition, and by the definition of the three pastors in this chapter.
2. Is the work complete?
3. What "hermeneutical lens" do you bring to the way you view the civil rights movement? What lenses do the pastors in this chapter bring?
4. Do we need another civil rights movement with a different focus? If so, what should that focus be? What did you think of the pastors' shared focus on prisons in America today?
5. Of what community groups are you a part (church, book group, League of Women Voters, Kiwanis, etc.)? How could your community group participate in a new civil rights movement?
6. What does the civil rights movement have to do with Beloved Community?

2

Border Battles

Can We Migrate into the Beloved Community?

"Thus says the Lord *of hosts, the God of Israel: Amend your ways and your doings, and let me dwell with you in this place. Do not trust in these deceptive words: 'This is the temple of the* Lord, *the temple of the* Lord, *the temple of the* Lord.'

"For if you truly amend your ways and your doings, if you truly act justly one with another, if you do not oppress the alien, the orphan, and the widow, or shed innocent blood in this place, and if you do not go after other gods to your own hurt, then I will dwell with you in this place, in the land that I gave of old to your ancestors forever and ever."

—Jeremiah 7:3–7 (nrsv)

"Whenever I start feeling too arrogant about myself, I always take a trip to America. The immigration guys kick the star out of stardom."

–Indian film superstar Shah Rukh Khan[1]

[1]"Shah Rukh Khan Detained Again on Arrival in New York," *Hollywood Reporter,* April 13, 2012, http://www.hollywoodreporter.com/news/shah-rukh-khan-detained-again-311705.

"Not like the brazen giant of Greek fame,
With conquering limbs astride from land to land;
Here at our sea-washed, sunset gates shall stand
A mighty woman with a torch, whose flame
Is the imprisoned lightning, and her name
Mother of Exiles. From her beacon-hand
Glows world-wide welcome; her mild eyes command
The air-bridged harbor that twin cities frame.
"Keep, ancient lands, your storied pomp!" cries she
With silent lips. "Give me your tired, your poor,
Your huddled masses yearning to breathe free,
The wretched refuse of your teeming shore.
Send these, the homeless, tempest-tost to me,
I lift my lamp beside the golden door!"

—"The Colossus," Emma Lazarus, 1883

The artwork Mary's getting known for is bright, vivid, and inspiring. It's the paintings from the Guadalupe Art Program, in colors that jump off the page and that you know have an amazing story behind them that you're dying to learn. She has another picture in her office, much more stark, much more challenging on its face. And it's telling the same story.

The Guadalupe Art Program started in San Diego, a city most of us associate with a zoo and wealthy people and nice beaches. It's also a border city. When Mary was a priest in San Diego, she started the Guadalupe Art Program because, in the Spanish-language ministry she ran, she encountered countless young women who were part of the rampant sex trafficking along our borders and across the country. As a way to help rebuild the dignity and divinity of the women—girls, really—she had them paint their own faces into artwork of the Virgin of Guadalupe. "There's a saying," she explains as a Mexican American herself, "Mexico is 90 percent Catholic, but it's 100 percent Guadalupano."[2] Imagine women who

[2]Gaudalupano: A believer in the Virgin Mary who showed herself to the Indigenous farmer Juan Diego in central Mexico in the 1500s. Part of the power of La Virgin de Guadalupe is that this is the first instance of her visiting a non-European.

had been forced into the sex trade (or women gang raped as their initiation into the gang that was their only safety and support group, or women in abusive relationships) getting to see themselves in the blessed virgin, getting to reclaim their wholeness and their dignity and their status as treasured daughters of God. The artwork is magnificent.

The other picture Mary has, though, is a photograph, not a painting. It is a picture of farm laborers—also trafficked across the border, or pushed across the border because there were no jobs where they lived and because we demand low-cost food that requires backbreaking labor at wages far lower than U.S. citizens will work for. The farm workers are sleeping on the highway underneath trucks, because there is nowhere else for them to sleep before their work begins. "Literally *on* the *highway*," she emphasizes.

Mary gets invited to speak about human trafficking a lot. The Guadalupe Art Program is powerful and inspiring and easy to understand. The thing is, there are more than a few places that this fifty-something Episcopal priest doesn't get invited back, because she won't only tell the story of the one picture; she tells the story of both. "I keep explaining that you can't understand human trafficking without also understanding immigration and incarceration and the war on drugs, and how they're all tied together," she explains. "And I get it. I don't think you can live in Oakland with your eyes open and not get it. But I also get that it is hard to help people make all of those connections without ruffling a lot of feathers."

La Reverenda, as her congregants sometimes call her, is willing to ruffle feathers. And because she recognizes that those bright, vibrant paintings that people clamor to see *and* the stark photo of the men sleeping under the truck tell the same story, ruffle feathers she does.

One time, Mary was given an award and asked to give a presentation on the Guadalupe Art Program. She started talking about how she met many of the teenage girls in prison because police arrested them for teenage prostitution. (Mary doesn't think we should be allowed to use the term "teenage prostitution," since it implies a level of agency that doesn't exist, and arresting the girls as the way to get them off the street is a horrifying way to protect them.) She talked about some of the other teenagers in prison and about migrant farm workers in the community. She was explaining their conditions—victims of sex trafficking, kids sucked into gangs because there were no alternatives, farm workers who would work all day and then when they were supposed to get paid would be chased away by bosses threatening to call immigration—when a woman interrupted her: "Are these people we're talking about ILLEGALS?" she asked loudly. Mary stared her down as seconds ticked by. "These are people who are victims of our economic system," she said, and continued her presentation.

That was one of the places Mary won't be invited back. She doesn't seem too bothered, as long as she keeps getting invited back to the women's shelter in San Francisco where she currently runs the Guadalupe Art Project with women escaping domestic violence or sex trafficking or avoiding a return to prison.

You sometimes hear immigration referred to as a "hot button issue." That is, a lot of people have really strong opinions on the subject of immigration in general and on undocumented immigration in particular.

I care about this issue as an immigrant myself, obviously. I became a U.S. citizen on an autumn morning in 1983. One of my favorite childhood memories is that the next morning, my pastor brought the newspaper clipping to use for the children's moment. I only now realize that when my pastor shared that picture, he was both modeling his deep love of the United States and the idea that this nation is great *because* of its immigrants. And he connected it to how Jesus loves and welcomes all people. (He did this in a farming/business congregation on the outskirts of Akron, Ohio, where that wouldn't have been a popular message if it hadn't been delivered by a retired Air Force Chaplain and about a precocious but beloved girl in pigtails who loved Jesus and sang really loudly during all the hymns.)

I also care about immigration as an avid reader and follower of U.S. history, which is littered with profound ambivalence about immigration from the top down. I find myself thinking of the furor during the 2014 Super Bowl when a soda company ran an ad with people singing "America the Beautiful" in multiple languages, and also of the popular Facebook meme with a Native American looking solidly at the camera with the following caption: "You don't like immigrants? Great. Let me help you pack your bags."

I think our ambivalence is both particular to the United States and incredibly universal. It is particular, since race has been shaped in very specific ways to create categories of who's in and who's out, categories that are constantly shifting. The Irish weren't "White" until they suddenly were.[3] People of Middle Eastern origin are considered White in census data but not in day-to-day life, making it impossible to track hate crimes effectively. It is only in the past twenty years that some states have gotten rid of the one-drop rule from states' classification systems that recorded anyone with 1/32 Black heritage or more as Black. Categories of race move correlative to economic needs in the nation.

It is universal because while our Scriptures repeat the biblical imperative to care for the sojourner dozens and dozens of times; I suspect that is because the ancient Israelites and then the early Christians, feeling threatened by outsiders, by people different from them, did not naturally *want* to help the outsiders. We all distrust people we don't know; it's instinctive. This is why to be a Christian demands that we stretch well beyond what is natural, beyond what is instinctive.

Mary's work is mostly about returning dignity to women and men who have had their dignity stripped away from them because our country has become dependent on cheap labor in order to enjoy low prices and great extravagance, or because some of us have decided we can have whatever we want whenever we want it. The economics of undocumented immigration are very complex, and I'm enough of a policy wonk that I could get really boring really quickly, so I will

---

[3]For great but hard reading on this subject, read Noel Ignatiev, *How the Irish Became White* (Milton Park, UK: Routledge Press, 1995).

make a few very broad generalizations and point you to a couple of articles that may be of interest.

- There are about 11 million undocumented immigrants in the United States. About 1/3 of them live in poverty, although almost all of them work. They come for a variety of reasons: to escape violence or threat to personal safety, to escape grinding poverty (often in countries where their homeland's relationship to the United States has contributed to their poverty) or so they can send money home to support family with no opportunities, and sometimes because they have been forced to come (sold or sent by families and then imprisoned and forced to work as slaves or to "work off" the cost of smuggling them into the United States).[4]
- Despite the media's portrayal of immigration as an issue strictly related to the U.S.-Mexico border, Mexican nationals make up only 55–60 percent of undocumented immigrants in the United States. This means 40–45 percent come from other countries,[5] including virtually all of the children that crossed our border in 2014, escaping the drug wars ravaging their countries, wars the United States unintentionally contributed to creating through both domestic and foreign policy around drugs and immigration and deportation.[6]
- Our economy is reliant on low wage jobs and hard labor, creating a market for illegally low wages for

[4]One of the most accessible resources on this subject, provided by the Morningside Center, is "Illegal Immigrants: Why do they come? What should the U.S. do about them?" by Alan Shapiro, with articles and case studies and activities. Available at: http://www.teachablemoment.org/high/immigration.html.

[5]For some perspective on what life is like for an Asian undocumented immigrant, read Zi Hem Ling, "For Asian Undocumented Immigrants, a Life of Secrecy," The Atlantic Monthly, May 14, 2013, http://www.theatlantic.com/national/archive/2013/05/for-asian-undocumented-immigrants-a-life-of-secrecy/275829/.

[6]For more about the child refugee crisis, read Sonia Nazario, "The children of the drug wars: A refugee crisis, not an immigration crisis," *The New York Times*, July 11, 2014, http://www.nytimes.com/2014/07/13/opinion/sunday/a-refugee-crisis-not-an-immigration-crisis.html?_r=0.

backbreaking work that U.S. citizens understand are far less than they deserve. When the state of Alabama created laws to push out all undocumented workers, crops rotted in the fields.[7] It is very difficult to foster a conversation on this, because at best our media might talk about whether illegal immigration is cost-effective for states or the federal government, but the economy is about far more than that; net costs and benefits are also about our grocery bills and CEOs' salaries and stock profits. In fact, those other things drive our laws more than the costs to taxpayers.[8]

- The term "illegal immigrant" was introduced in the early 1990s for very political reasons. When we insist on using the term "undocumented immigrants" (with the accompanying declaration, "No human being is illegal"), we often get decried for not telling the truth. But, as the points above indicate, I believe that it is immoral to simultaneously blame immigrants while leaving completely unquestioned an economic system in the United grounded in the exploitation of workers to such an extent that it would fall apart if underpaid and overworked (or functionally enslaved) persons were not part of that system.[9]
- In recent history, this has happened repeatedly: when cheap Chinese labor for the railroads was no longer needed, anti-Chinese legislation emerged in the late 1800s. The resulting dearth of low-income

---

[7]A narrative of immigrants and the farm workers who employ them: Paul Reyes, "'It's Just Not Right': The Failures of Alabama's Self-Deportation Experiment," *Mother Jones Magazine,* March/April 2012. Available at: http://www.motherjones.com/politics/2012/03/alabama-anti-immigration-law-self-deportation-movement.

[8]An illustration of my point is this very interesting *New York Times* article that looks at illegal immigration from a cost-benefit perspective but assumes that cost to taxpayers is the primary issue at stake: Adam Davidson, "Do Illegal Immigrants Actually Hurt the US Economy?" *New York Times Magazine,* February 12, 2013. Available at: http://www.nytimes.com/2013/02/17/magazine/do-illegal-immigrants-actually-hurt-the-us-economy.html?pagewanted=all&_r=0.

[9]Journalist Jose Vargas offered a great Ted Talk on the issue of this term, "I Am an Illegal Immigrant," in April 2013. Available at: http://blog.ted.com/2013/04/08/rethinking-the-term-illegal-immigrant-because-people-cant-be-illegal/. He also recently made an excellent film called *Documented.*

> workers was filled by Japanese immigrants although their rights were severely curtailed, then the Bracero program of Mexican guest workers, and so on. (The complex relationship of labor unions to immigrants is directly connected to the economic system that relies on cheap labor and exploitation; for decades, poor American workers of all races have been pitted against immigrants.)[10]

Francisca isn't particularly religious, and she's not an artist. But her work is almost identical to that of Mary, although she does it on picket lines these days instead of in a church or art room.

I met Francisca when a handful of religious leaders joined with some workers protesting the Castlewood Golf Club in Pleasanton, California. The management had locked out some workers for not agreeing to a new contract where the workers had to pay all of their own health care (consuming up to 40 percent of some employees' paychecks) in what the club had described as a record-breaking earnings year. I didn't learn it until later, but Francisca was the janitor who had found a memo in the new manager's trash can saying that his primary objective was to shut down the union (which had functioned without any conflict for over twenty years). And fight they did, almost imperiling the future of the club out of management's belief in their right to not provide health care or fair wages.

What struck me about this campaign was that the union working with them had assumed U.S. citizens would be the most upset and willing to stand up for fair treatment. Instead, it was mostly immigrants, including undocumented immigrants, who stood on the picket line for month after month. "Most of the white people had good positions, like

---

[10]*Network*, a Catholic social justice organization, provides a brief summary of the history of immigration, available at: http://www.networklobby.org/history-immigration. To specifically learn about the Bracero program, the Southern Poverty Law Center has provided a helpful summary, available at: http://www.splcenter.org/publications/close-to-slavery-guestworker-programs-in-the-united-states/a-brief-history-of-guestwork.

bartender," Francisca explains. "The only two white people on our side, it was just because they knew better. One day one member told Miss Peggy, 'You old hog; go home and die.' We grew a thick skin. We Mexicans put up with everything. I told people I put Vaseline on my face every morning so what they would say will slide off me."

Most of the workers on the picket line were from the kitchen or served as janitors. They were mostly Latin@. When Francisca reached out to one of the White servers to join their protest of the unfair working conditions, he responded, "With all due respect, what am I going to do there? I'm in front of the members serving them their food. If I join you, they're going to know who I am. And with all due respect, it's a bunch of Mexicans and Michael and Peggy."

Francisca's Vaseline didn't work for everyone. One of the cooks on the picket line knew every member by name and how they liked their food prepared. He would literally cry most days at how the members treated the picketers, saying he thought they were his friends. The hostility of most club members was devastating to him after so many years of knowing them so well. "We used to joke that we needed to chip in for Carlos to get therapy, because he really thought they were his friends and every day he was in tears. We told him, 'The only thing they care about is if the new person knows how they like their sandwich. We're just Mexicans; they don't care. The day one of them asks if you have enough for rent, you can tell if they care.'" Then Francisca noted, "One of the members who did care and helped us—they wanted to throw him out." (A few other members did help but insisted that the workers tell no one; they did not want to experience the same ostracism.)

Francisca wants to see the Mexican community work together in America, saying sometimes what she sees is people competing, stepping on each other to get ahead, and that's not right. That was part of why, although her previous experience with a union had been a bad one, and although she was a documented resident who could have given up and looked for another job, she stayed and joined the struggle:

"If we didn't do anything, there was going to be over forty families on the street. A lot of cooks, if they earned $16 an hour at Castlewood, they were earning $8 an hour in a new place." In this part of the country, $16 an hour is not a ton, but some of the people locked out of their jobs were supporting family here or abroad on that salary: "In the dishwashing department, at least five people." Their spouses and kids were in Mexico and they were trying to give them a better future with education. In Mexico you have to buy everything to go to school, so they were trying to give their kids a better education. Families were struggling to make ends meet. People were helping their mothers who were elderly, too."

Francisca reminded me of an issue we don't always talk about when weighing the technical aspects of immigration: "Most people who come to this country, when they come across the border, you need to think of the dangers they face. They're forced to come here because things are so bad in their country; it's hard to feed their families and government doesn't help. It's hard even if you have an education. People are just looking for a better future for themselves. Coming here and being treated like this is just really hard."

On the picket line one day, a member bicycled by with a stroller attached in back. As they biked by, the toddler stuck its hand out of its fabric enclosure and gave the workers a "thumbs down." The mother turned around and biked by again, and the toddler stuck out the other hand to do the same thing. I'm partly just impressed by the commitment to biking in such uneven terrain just to get your kid to harass picketers, but Francisca noted that the saddest thing to her was a parent teaching her child to hate because "we were on their land." (Maybe it's because I'm an immigrant or maybe it's because I'm a Christian, but the notion that any of us have the right to claim stolen land as ours more than the people working it is a weird one to me.)

I joined the workers in a three-day fast over Mother's Day weekend, where they tried to remind club members that many of the workers were mothers or were supporting mothers, and that this protest was taking food out of the mouths of mothers and children. On Mother's Day, the fasting protesters stood quietly with flyers about the conflict with management, and a woman came up to another worker, Maria (who had adopted two little children two days before she was locked out of her job; the theme of this weekend was very personal to her) and spat at Maria, "You are TEARING APART FAMILIES!" The woman's son had refused to eat at the country club for Mother's Day because of the workers' protest. Maria had to work really hard to extend Christian love in response (although by then the workers were used to being catcalled and threatened with phone calls to Immigration and jeers to go back to Mexico).

Francisca had to fight the urge to not yell back, "Because, when you go back you need to go back with your head held high. They also called us uneducated and dumb and you don't know what you're fighting for. I wanted to be able to show them who had the education. I knew we were going back and I wanted to be able to look people in their eyes and not be ashamed."

I came here when I was a toddler. I get complimented regularly on having "no accent." (I do have an accent. I have an American accent.) I came here because my father's friend in England moved to the United States and opened some doors for my father to get a good job at Firestone in Akron. Firestone helped with our documentation process. I can never be President of the United States. Otherwise, other than occasionally having to provide some extra paperwork that U.S.-born citizens don't have to and possibly being on a watch list somewhere (9/11 has some funny blowback for some of us), immigration issues don't impact me much anymore.

Those issues didn't affect Moses too much, either. He spent most of his life thinking he was a high-ranking Egyptian, and then he ended up becoming the leader of his actual people, the Israelites. But brother married a Midianite. Leviticus and Deuteronomy have so many injunctions against cruel treatment of non-Israelites who pass through their territory. Sometimes I wonder if that has anything to do with the fact that their greatest leader reminded them to extend compassion to sojourners wandering through. After all, the Midianites had shown him that compassion, and the Israelites also didn't want to replicate the brutality they had experienced in Egypt for generations, did they?

A generation of incredibly courageous young people began changing the face of immigration conversations a couple of years back. Their nickname is the Dreamers because they have been trying since 2001 to pass the DREAM Act (**D**evelopment, **R**elief, and **E**ducation for **A**lien **M**inors, originally proposed by liberal Democrat Dick Durbin of Illinois and conservative Republican Orrin Hatch of Utah), and I've had the chance to know and hear the stories of some of them. They're the young adults who were brought into the country at a young age without documents and have lived here ever since, seeking the right to stay here legally and be able to go to college and live their lives publicly instead of staying hidden. They have risked arrest and deportation in huge numbers to bring attention to the lack of humanity of the immigration system. I have watched people explain to them that on a system-wide level, it's not fair to let them stay in the country, but when those same people hear the Dreamers' stories, they can find no way to argue that our nation's constitution would want them to be deported. They can find even less of a way to argue that it would be a morally justified decision. And in the face of a Congress determined to be unyielding in regards to immigration, the Dreamers gave President Obama the moral courage in 2012 to pass Deferred Action for Childhood Arrivals that allows those undocumented immigrants under the age of twenty-eight who came here as children to apply for permanent residency. Their courageous and risk-taking work and the faces of the children coming to the United States as refugees from drug wars in central America are forcing us to have conversations about morality, compassion, and justice that we should already have been having, that Moses would call on us as fellow sojourners to have.

Rev. Dr. Alvin Jackson was the reason I became a Disciple of Christ, and I still consider him my pastor. I remember him, an African American addressing a mixed group of White and Latin@ and Asian people and saying of America, "We may have come over on different ships, but we're all in the same boat now." Some of us actually inhabited this land for thousands of years, but most of our forebears came here as slaves or indentured servants, or they came here to establish a better life. Like the Israelites, we came onto others' land by choice or by force and had to find rules to live by that honored each other and hopefully created a better place for all of us. Like the Israelites, we did better by some people than others, and we did best when we were ruled by hope rather than by fear.

But Dr. Jackson is still right: we're all in the same boat now. Mary and Francisca are helping all of us remember that as we build a Beloved Community together, we make sure that all people's work is honored, that no one's work is forced or exploited, and that we do not step over each other to get a better position. Mary does it with art and Francisca does it with protest chants, but both of them help us build a Beloved Community of less exploitation, deeper acknowledgment of one another's humanity, and greater compassion.

CHAPTER QUESTIONS

1. If you are part of a worshiping community, where did the ancestors of the members of your congregation come from?
2. Where did your ancestors come from? What challenges did they face in becoming part of the American fabric? Where do you see similarities between their story and the story of the people in this chapter?
3. Where are the immigrants in your town from?
4. Does your congregation have any programs they share with immigrant groups? If not, could some be devised? Are there homework help or English language classes your church could help with or sponsor?

5. What interactions have you had with immigrants? How does this chapter make you think about the immigrants you interact with differently? (Or what does it reinforce?)
6. What discussions have you engaged in about the refugee children coming across the U.S. border to flee drug wars in several Central American countries? How does scripture speak to their situation and ours?
7. What does immigration have to do with the Beloved Community?

3

Murky Terminology

"In this country American means white. Everybody else has to hyphenate."

—Toni Morrison

"Pit race against race, religion against religion, prejudice against prejudice. Divide and conquer! We must not let that happen here."

—Eleanor Roosevelt

"Now during those days, when the disciples were increasing in number, the Hellenists complained against the Hebrews because their widows were being neglected in the daily distribution of food. And the twelve called together the whole community of the disciples and said, 'It is not right that we should neglect the word of God in order to wait on tables. Therefore, friends, select from among yourselves seven men of good standing, full of the Spirit and of wisdom, whom we may appoint to this task, while we, for our part, will devote ourselves to prayer and to serving the word.' What they said pleased the whole community, and they chose Stephen, a man full of faith and the Holy Spirit, together with Philip, Prochorus, Nicanor, Timon, Parmenas, and Nicolaus, a proselyte of Antioch. They had these men stand before the apostles, who prayed and laid their hands on them."

—Acts 6:1–6 (NRSV)

Welton had already engaged in the issue of racial justice a fair bit by the time he was dean at a seminary in Kentucky for Black ministers in training who could not attend a traditional seminary. He was serving there the day Martin Luther King Jr. was shot.

A White man born into the Jim Crow South of Tennessee, Rev. Dr. Welton Gaddy received the complex and multilayered messages of his location and era: he grew up on the "wrong side of town" and had Black playmates while simultaneously seeing images of "the Happy Negro," the contented southern African American who was happy with his life. (When Phil Robinson from the television show *Duck Dynasty* was swept up in December of 2013 in a scandal primarily for his comments about God condemning homosexuality, he alluded to this same trope, incorrectly stating that Black people were happier before the end of Jim Crow because they had God and values then.) He also grew up in the era of the ascendancy of television where images of the bus boycott and the early days of the civil rights movement gave lie to that comforting image.

Welton grew up in segregated schools and remembers the Supreme Court Case Brown v. Board of Education that proclaimed *Separate but Equal is Not Equal*. "And I remember beginning to ask my parents about what kind of schools Black people went to in our town," remembers Welton. "And they had bought the idea that the schools were equal. Then when the civil rights movement began in its earliest forms, I began to see a fear in a lot of the people who were racist that things were going to change. I remember the fear mongering that went on, with people saying if the Supreme Court stays true to what they're doing, they're going to ruin the country. That's when the racist ministers in the country started using the Bible to put down Black people with all sorts of methods of biblical interpretation. I remember one that stuck in my dad's mind: in nature you don't see a crossover between animals and birds and they stay to their own species. That had made me conscious of the importance of race."

Welton went to a seminary where an ethics professor helped him realize that the Bible spoke powerfully to racial justice, after having been raised in a Southern Baptist Church that did not always preach that message. In his earliest days of preaching, when it was not popular, Welton said he preached to the congregation that had raised him, "You all taught me the song *Jesus loves the little children of the world*. You said red and yellow, black and white. I don't think you meant it, so why did you teach me that?" Welton goes on to say, "When I moved past, 'You lied to me and I resent it,' I started to preach on the book of Acts. One of the great challenges of the church was to discover whether it was really discriminatory in relationship to Jews and Gentiles and the contributions in relation to Peter and Cornelius were just outline points for talking on race."

So Welton already got the importance of racial justice and had been working to address it for years when he had to face his all-Black class on the morning of April 5, 1968, the morning after Dr. King was shot in Memphis, Tennessee. He walked into the class where the students were supposed to take an exam and said, "We're just going to talk this morning; no exam. We're just going to be with each other."

Dr. King's brother lived in Memphis, where Welton was teaching, and, as Welton remembers, "Most of them said, 'We've been over at Mr. King's house and we've been praying.' 'What have you been praying about?' 'We've been praying for the King family and we've been praying for the man who shot him.' And I found myself thinking, 'Something about this spirituality—there's something there we [White people] did not get.'"

To me, that's the point in Welton's story when he stopped focusing primarily on racial justice and started focusing on racism. That's a pretty nuanced claim, and one that I'm making in Welton's behalf.

Part of what's tricky about conversations on race is the constantly moving target that is the definitions we use. "I don't mean to be racist," I overheard a young Black man say to a Latino security officer one morning, before continuing, "but I wanna *throw* something at a Mexican, I'm so mad right now."

"Everyone's a little bit racist," goes a song in the Gen X musical *Avenue Q*.

"You want to talk about racism?" my mother asks. "Let's talk about most of the ESL (English as a Second Language) students I teach. The Latino students are always talking about Black people being lazy and dirty. The number of times I've had to give the tuba player speech." (My mother's tuba player speech is about stereotyping and goes like this: "What can you say that is true of all tuba players?" People often say things like, "They're large," "They love music," or, "They have back problems from carrying those instruments." Her response: "The only thing you can say that is true of all tuba players is that they all play the tuba.")

I want to share Welton's story partly because I think we're all in this struggle together, "Red and Yellow, Black and White" (as problematic as that song now is), and partly because it gives me an excuse to clarify some terms I'll be using in this book (but that I think would be helpful for us to use in general because our inconsistent definitions do us few favors in the work for dignity and equality and full relationship of all of God's children).

Hence my plunge into two terms most people use interchangeably. To me, ***racial justice*** is about recognizing that *all people deserve the same rights* regardless of race, and *advocating for policies* to change to represent that. Abraham Lincoln moved racial justice forward, although he did not profess that Black people were equal to White people. Martin Luther King did publicly profess that Black and White people (and Vietnamese people) were equal in God's sight, but as he moved further into the movement and found hearts and minds couldn't always be moved, he did not give up on a policy of racial justice in law. When asked why he didn't focus primarily on hearts and minds, he famously responded, "It may be true that the law cannot make a man love me, but it can keep him from lynching me, and I think that's pretty important."

Abraham Lincoln was an advocate of racial justice in law, but he clearly had some race prejudice in him that was part of the culture of his era, having publicly stated that he believed there were biological differences between Black and White races that prohibited political or legal equality. The students my mother works with also have race prejudice: most of them were taught that Black people are lazy and dirty through exposure to U.S. media and common stereotypes that get circulated without ever having to meet a Black person (and certainly without having met all of them, so as to challenge their tuba player assumptions). I have ***race prejudices*** that I've absorbed. I try hard to overcome them when I'm conscious of them, but, man, are they baked in! (My irreverent sense of humor has alluded to repressed English people, overly celebratory Filipinos, and snobbish Bengalis just in the two hours before I wrote this.) You may have gone through racial sensitivity, cultural sensitivity, or cultural competence training to address some of these issues in your workplace.

Racism, on the other hand, goes deeper even than policies and deeper than the stereotypes and biases we've absorbed personally. Racism, as I use the definition throughout this book, is the combination of race prejudice that we've all soaked up and power within systems and institutions. So it's kind of a soup of the things we've been talking about: there are policies in this country that were created by people with power and are embedded in our systems and institutions. Those systems and institutions within themselves have power, right? (If you don't agree, try not paying your taxes. The IRS is definitely an institution with power.) And the people who created policies and built systems and institutions were functioning out of race prejudice, just like we all do. The difference is, their race prejudice had power behind it so it shapes all of our lives. The equation, which you might have seen before, is this:

RACISM = RACE PREJUDICE + POWER

Now I think these definitions matter a lot because we often talk past each other when talking about race, and we're often not even sure of why. My mother has a very succinct way of putting it (helped by being White but also being an immigrant, I think): "White people tend to look back and see how far we've come; people of color are daily reminded of how far we have to go."

And I think part of why we talk past each other has to do with the last part of that equation: *power*. I realized I wanted to address definitions after reading this very popular blog post in August 2013 from the website *Everyday Feminism* called "That's Racist Against White People! A Discussion on Power and Privilege,"[1] which says in part, "Too often, when people are talking about racism or sexism or heterosexism or any other form of oppression, they're simply referring to when a person was made to feel bad for or about their identity. **There is absolutely *no* acknowledgement of wider systems of oppression and power.** And that is no accident."

Some people are aware of power, and particularly power by systems and institutions and how that helps some and hurts others. However, many people have not been made aware that they do have any power in this particular arena of race, or they don't think of how that changes the impact of their race prejudice as compared with others' (if they're able to acknowledge they've soaked up any race prejudice in the first place). So a lot of people use the word "racism" to describe what I'm calling "race prejudice." If the writers of *Avenue Q* had asked my editorial advice, I might have rewritten their popular song to go, "Everyone's a little bit race prejudiced, but real racism takes power!" (It sounds better when sung by puppets.)

And all of this leads to another phrase I'll use throughout the book that might make the reader incredibly uncomfortable; it's taken me years to get comfortable saying it because it carries more power than a curse word in some circles: ***White privilege***. This phrase can be a conversation ender, and I try to use it judiciously. It's another phrase that people interpret in lots of different ways. Here's what I mean by it: because of these systems and institutions that perpetuate racism, certain

---

[1]Available at: http://everydayfeminism.com/2013/08/racist-against-white-people/.

groups get privileged and helped while other groups get harmed and disadvantaged. What this looks like for a White person is, for example, that they receive privileges they didn't ask for: if they get arrested for the exact same crime as a Black person, they are statistically likely to get a markedly lighter sentence.[2] A White person gets to drive through Arizona or Alabama knowing that s/he will not get pulled over by police for "looking like an immigrant," even though this country has a large number of White immigrants, many of whom are undocumented. The list of privileges that White people don't ask for but receive is a long one. And it's a less frequently discussed issue than the harm to people of color that is addressed by racial justice, but it is equally powerful in keeping racism in place and having power over all of us.

For many, Ferguson was a game changer because it brought into critical relief issues of systemic racism that target one race and preserve privilege for another. As someone living in a community constantly engaging questions about police brutality against people of color (the city of Oakland was forced several years ago to receive federal oversight of our legendarily unaccountable police department, and the film *Fruitvale Station* brought national attention to the issue—during Occupy Oakland, protesters renamed the plaza in front of city hall "Oscar Grant Plaza" after the young father killed by public transit police on New Year's Day in 2012), I recognized it as a bellwether issue in a campaign many people of color have been fighting for years now. The #BlackLivesMatter campaign had already emerged after Trayvon Martin's murder.[3] Possibly this was simply the moment that young White people really began to take the issue seriously as well. And that in and of itself is part of the

---

[2]This issue has been discussed extensively in Michelle Alexander's groundbreaking book *The New Jim Crow* (2010; repr., New York: The New Press, 2012), which focuses on harm to the Black community but is simultaneously fed by White privilege in both disparate sentencing between Blacks and Whites and the financial benefit from the prison industrial complex primarily benefiting the White community.

[3]Alicia Garza, "A Herstory of the #BlackLivesMatter Movement," October 7, 2014, http://thefeministwire.com/2014/10/blacklivesmatter-2/.

power of racism: it has the power to isolate us from each other so that something deeply impacting one group's lives for years only fully enters the consciousness of another group when the media is forced to cover the issue.

For those of us in the Christian community, though, this will always be both an issue of just policies and also of hearts and minds, because we are about the work of building up the realm of God. This is really well illustrated by Welton's reflection on how he talked about engaging civil rights in the church in the 1960s: "I probably did not use the word *justice* much in those days. It was far more personal than that. But the whole matter of equality in education and marriage, the inequity of economics of race all began to come to the fore. I would go at it then when I did thematic preaching. I tried not imposingly but with I hope some finesse to talk with these farmers with whom I had little in common, frankly. I remember one [occasion] where we had a long and heated discussion on race and I finally said, 'I'm sorry; we've talked too long.' And he said, 'Don't worry about it; it's better than talking about the crops.'"

So I lift up these definitions because I think they're helpful for having a clearer conversation, and because I think part of how racism retains a hold on us even though we don't want it to is that we don't have the vocabulary for the conversation. I also remember that what matters more is God's children—*all* of God's children—being fully known and being full participants side-by-side in the building of God's realm. So when the words get in the way of the conversation, let's stay at the table and find the words that move us forward. And let's never underestimate one another's capacity to engage in this dialogue, because it might just be better than talking about the crops.

Because we want to be a loving family and because many of us have been taught that tension should be avoided to preserve peace, conversations about race can be particularly hard to have in the church. If we could embrace the notion that disagreement is a healthy part of a loving family, we might be able to move the ball much further down the field, as Welton learned in his own life: "My parents and I had a relationship in which we talked about most everything; the most lively arguments I've ever had were with my mother and dad over race. Fortunately we had the commonality of loving each other so we were very honest with each other, but I think we made some progress. That was a good training ground for me because by the time I was having it with church members, the passion was there but I also knew how to control it."

Welton was interested in controlling it because he was in this out of love for all of God's children, even the ones who weren't where he was: "There was always a willingness to engage that kind of prejudice. The argument at this point was, 'This is not an immoral South.' This is much more a cultural issue than a spiritual or moral issue. I had to say if the culture is encouraging immorality, the culture is wrong and we have to change it."

Part of how Welton learned his role and responsibilities in relationship to the Black community was through the dialogue the church so often fears: "I remember sitting down in a community center and talking with an older Black guy who asked if I was prejudiced, and I said no, and he explained to me why I was. One of the derivatives of that story was that what is absolutely essential in discussions of race is honesty and holding each other to be honest. It doesn't work if everyone involved isn't honest."

And with this knowledge from his relationships in the Black community and because of Welton's White privilege and because of his relationships, people listened to him who wouldn't have listened to a person of color or even a stranger, and he was able to convey experiences of people who would not otherwise have been heard in the rooms into which Welton could walk.

This is a good illustration of the one other term I want to add to the mix: ***ally***. Welton has a lot of privilege, and he is fully aware of that. Instead of trying to hide that privilege or trying to pretend he doesn't have it, Welton uses it to move forward work that others wouldn't be able to move forward. The reason I know Welton is that I used to work for him at The Interfaith Alliance, where it made a pretty big impact having a tall and imposing White (former) Southern Baptist preacher take the mike at a press conference and, in his eloquent and simultaneously Southern-inflected turn of phrase, speak out for the rights of persecuted South Asian and Middle Eastern Muslims, Sikhs, and Hindus in the wake of 9/11, for example (both in policy and practice). That's what it looks like to choose to be an ally: to use one's power to support people who don't benefit from the same privilege and who experience marginalization, while having the relationships and humility to first listen to the people from those marginalized communities and then create space for their voices.

The reason Welton does this has everything to do with his commitment to God's kin-dom: "I came out of those seminary classes thinking the credibility of Christianity is at stake. If we prove ourselves exclusive and racist then we've lost our credibility."

I asked Welton if there were any costs to being an ally as public as he was, and he said circumspectly, "There were costs, but I can honestly say I don't think I ever—if I did I've forgotten—but I don't think I ever sat around and worried about the consequences of that message. Well, when I was a pastor in Louisville, somebody shot a bottle rocket at me while I was in the pulpit. I don't know whether that was about race." He laughed. Then he shared the stories of people he worked with for whom the pressure of their very brave work resulted in dire consequences. For example, a man in east Tennessee who walked Black children into a school when it was first integrated ended up taking his own life. Another man in North Carolina who stood for civil rights had his house shot up (presumably by the Klan) and had to flee the town for his life.

When I worked with Welton at The Interfaith Alliance, he was part of the team that worked on the religious statement on racism that was part of President Clinton's Town Halls on Race all across the country. He gained traction and a little notoriety on the issue of the religious community's response to racism when he was asked to draft the statement for that group. "What I remember most was the conversations I had with people in the evangelical community because I wrote that racism was a sin and they didn't want me to use that word; I balked. If I'm writing it, it's going to be said. Whether they meant this or not, I read that as, 'Let's don't call it sin because it's not as bad as what we usually call sin,' and my opinion was, 'That is why we need to call it that; because it's equally evil and probably more evil than what evangelicals usually call sin.'"

This actually points to the thing I wanted to lift up at the beginning of this chapter, but I let it roll to the end: Welton's commitment to the core message of the Bible is a guiding force in his work for racial justice, and it stems back to his earliest days in the Southern Baptists: "The one thing that stayed with me even to this point from my childhood religion and instruction is to take the Bible seriously. And with some education I determined that interpreting the Bible was important. Never, after a little education, did I interpret the Bible literally. But to this day I interpret the Bible seriously."

One of the books of the Bible Welton takes seriously is also a really important one to me: the book of Acts, a tale of how the early church found its feet—stories of great achievements and experiments gone awry and people of deep loyalty and people who were deeply human. As I think about the many definitions I've dropped in the reader's lap, I find myself thinking about a particular story from the book of Acts. The church's center was in Jerusalem. And part of being church, they figured out almost immediately, was providing for orphans and widows who were neglected in society at the time. Probably all widows got about the same amount of food, but at some point the women who had come to Jerusalem from abroad (the women from the Diaspora) complained that the widows from Jerusalem were getting more food. I heard a Latino missiology professor from Fuller Seminary once speak to this passage. As I recall, he said that probably everyone got the same basic food, but the people running the food distribution would know the cousin of the niece of this particular local widow and slip her an extra slice of the fancy coffee cake since there wasn't enough for everyone to get that particular special dish. There was no malice, there was no intention of underfeeding some to overfeed others, but you give the little perks to the people you're connected with. Peter's solution to this complaint: place the Diasporic community in charge of creating a system of food distribution that doesn't prefer anyone.

Peter had a lot of power in that situation, and he was a man of Jerusalem. I love that the early church, wrestling with some of the same things we face, modeled some very unconventional thinking for our sake. They acknowledged where power and privilege resided so that they could subvert that power and instead let God's power reign supreme over them all equally. That was a glimpse of the Beloved Community: honesty, humility, and equity.

As I picture the Beloved Community today, I can imagine how relationships in the church would eventually become richer and deeper as people work together to create true equity. And I think it would look a little like Welton learning from a Black man in Tennessee why Welton was actually prejudiced, and taking that knowledge to his own community for the sake of reconciliation.

CHAPTER QUESTIONS:

1. Is the community where your congregation is situated a multicultural and multiracial community? Is this diversity seen in your congregation? Looking at the definitions in this chapter, do you have any thoughts on why there is or is not diversity in your congregation?
2. How is your congregation is reaching out to the community?
3. How might a church in a nondiverse neighborhood can teach about diverse cultures and races?
4. Are there different places of worship nearby that could be visited by a class or youth group?

5. How does the provided definition of racism (racism = race prejudice + misuse of power) cause you to think about the situation in Ferguson, the DREAM Act, or other issues that came up in previous chapters?
6. What do anti-racism, cultural competency, and racial justice have to do with the Beloved Community?

4

(The Myth of) The Angry Black Man

"As an African American man aware of the historical treatment of African Americans, it would be fair to conclude that we have every right and reason to be enraged. In fact if you don't have rage you're not paying attention. We are persona non grata in America. We are asked to accept the fact that we are unacceptable. We are told constantly, 'Nothing you do will be accepted, but you need to keep doing everything you can to be accepted.' The moment you stop trying to be accepted, you're an angry black man."

–Servant B.K. Woodson, Sr.

"As they led him away, they seized a man, Simon of Cyrene, who was coming from the country, and they laid the cross on him, and made him carry it behind Jesus."

–Luke 23:26 (NRSV)

When I told B.K. that I wanted to interview him for a chapter on the myth of the angry Black man, I could see the gleam in his eye as he said, "You know what the myth of the Angry Black Man is, right?"

"Yeah, I know, he has every right to be angry," I said, trying not to sound blasé. Don't get me wrong—I came up with the chapter, and it's true. It's just that within certain circles it's become a truism just barely bordering on hackneyed.

Before I could even quite finish, he said, "The myth is—you see, the myth isn't that we're angry. The myth is bigger: that anger keeps us alive; it's a survival technique in the midst of all the horrors and indignities we face. And it's what is killing us too."

B.K. is a cerebral brother.

Servant Brian K. Woodson, Sr. was born two years after Emmett Till, a Black Chicago teen, was killed by a white mob while visiting family in the South for allegedly whistling at a White woman in 1955. He grew up as the civil rights movement blossomed and flourished and evolved. His family integrated a Lutheran school in Glendale, Queens, and his childhood notions of God were formed in a Reformed Church of America congregation in the heart of what had become a Black ghetto in Brooklyn. So he would move from his home and friends and family in Brooklyn where every face looked like his, and within two subway rides and a bus, his would be the only Black face in a sea of White.

I asked B.K. whether he remembered being angry much as a young man, and he talked about how he could walk down the street and pass these big guys recently released from Attica and back on the streets of the neighborhood, and sometimes he'd look down and just walk around them. Other times the anger inside him would drive him straight toward them. And the code in Brooklyn was you didn't walk into a fight unless you were prepared, if necessary, to kill someone or die trying. When I asked him what that was about, he said, "I don't know; life and death, rage. I don't know." I was immediately taken to my work in south Los Angeles in the early 2000s where I worked with formerly incarcerated men, mostly Latino, all gang affiliated. Good guys without a lot of options, mostly. And I remembered affirming one of the guys for choosing not to get involved in a revenge killing, which he would have done without a moment's hesitation except that his girlfriend was pregnant and he had decided he wanted to be around for his child. My mentor told me that one guy we worked with had shot someone in the neighborhood one night in a gang shootout, and then didn't drive, but *bicycled* through the neighborhood the next day in broad daylight, right down the middle of the street. "Suicidal tendencies masked by homicidal behaviors" was the term he used. So how does someone get to a place like that?

B.K. shared a story from his childhood, and you can picture it: The kids have taken over a block of a quiet street in pre-gentrification Brooklyn so they can play football. It's the kind of thing you see in movies nostalgic for a bucolic and innocent day gone by. B.K. is seven or eight. His mom works as a guidance counselor for the public schools and his dad works as a police officer for the Port Authority of New York/New Jersey. He doesn't have a ton to worry about as he throws and catches with the other kids. A cop car rolls up, not that different, maybe, than the one his dad drives at work. The cop rolls down the window and out of the blue shouts at eight-year-old Brian, "You better get out of the m----- f---ing street or I'll break your f---ing arm." And that's a day in the life of a Black kid in Brooklyn in the 1960s.

A few years later B.K. remembers watching a man talking to a police officer on his corner, "And as soon as the backup sirens are close enough to hear, the cop starts beating the guy, just wailing on him." The other cops arrive and join the beating. There are people on the street saying to each other that this is wrong, and someone gets up the courage to shout, "I'll talk to a sergeant." One of the backup cops pulls him to the side, puts the billy club in his face and says, "You shut your f---ing mouth or you'll get the same thing."

"These," B.K. muses, "are the seeds of hatred."

A world of few choices and constant degradation is something you probably must have actually experienced to fully understand. A lot of Americans have no idea the gauntlet that some Americans face every day. The fancy term is "microaggression": all the ways a Black man is made to feel less than—from the way women clutch their purses as he walks by to the way people don't hear the idea he brings up in a meeting until a White person says the exact same thing to the way he might get described as "articulate," unconsciously suggesting a certain surprise that a Black man would be able to speak like a well-educated White man. Philosopher, hip hop drummer, and dreamboat QuestLove wrote an op-ed after George Zimmerman's acquittal in the killing of Black teenager Trayvon Martin in which he said that as he got into the elevator with an attractive White woman at his high-end apartment building in New York. He asked for her floor number to press the button for her, and she didn't say anything. He thought to himself, "Beautiful lady living on my floor! Excellent!" When he stepped off the elevator, she stayed on. She had been afraid to let him know what floor she lived on.

When I told B.K. this story and used the term microaggression, he responded, "I call it the ubiquitous benign hatred that African Americans are subjected to. It's all the time, but if you point out every little thing people will say, 'Really? You're gonna get upset about something like that?' Microaggression has a ring of legitimacy to it. To me it's just hatred. It's denying my humanity."

And when the message is repeatedly that you have no value, the hurt and anger can turn inward or it can turn outward. For B.K. it turned outward (and maybe inward at the same time): by getting involved in civil rights campaigns as early as the age of ten, by facing down ex-cons as he walked through his neighborhood, and by joining the military. I wonder a tiny bit if God calling him to ministry (in a White denomination) might have provided the one healthy channel for his anger that wouldn't get him killed. And, in the process, he has been a gift to communities of all sorts—B.K. stands on the side of everyone who is being hurt and everyone who is doing good, regardless of race, gender, or orientation. And, fair enough, he's usually a little angry whenever he's standing at your side, but he's angry at injustice. So, particularly as a people who follow a book whose content is made up of about fifty percent righteous anger (hello, prophets; hello, Paul; hello, God dealing with the Israelites in the wilderness) and a Savior who overturned the tables in the temple because poor people were being manipulated by the moneychangers, why are we trained to be afraid of that anger when it is in the manifestation of a Black man?[1]

A lot of people like to chat with me about Black/White race issues because I'm not Black and only kind of White (depending on who you ask), so I'm a neutral third party (kind of like when comedian W. Kamau Bell sought to solve the generational debate about pumpkin pie versus sweet potato pie and used a blindfolded panel of a Latina, an East Asian man, and a South Asian woman to resolve the dispute. Sweet potato pie won 2-1). I get questions about why the term "articulate" is offensive when it's a compliment and why we have to keep talking about slavery. But a question I get asked more than any other by White people is, "Don't they realize they're hurting their cause when they're angry all the time?" Or—and this tends to come from liberal White allies—"Don't they understand nonviolence is the only real solution?" usually after windows have been broken in downtown Oakland in the wake of another injustice against a young Black man.

I'm an advocate of nonviolence in all situations for theological as well as strategic reasons. And I remember the night that the George Zimmerman verdict came down. One of my closest friends, a young Black man who is also a devout Quaker, said, "I have never wanted to cause damage so much in my whole life." Some people's knee-jerk reaction was, "Don't do that!" or, "That won't solve anything."

And I started to get what is broken in our paradigm. Many people's first reaction to my friend's statement wasn't, "This must feel awful. I'm outraged, too." It was more worried about his anger than about what provoked his anger. It wasn't seeking to understand why he felt that way.

And we missed a theological opportunity.

---

[1]Since the non-indictments of officers in the deaths of Michael Brown and Eric Garner at the end of 2014, a variation on that question has emerged in my community, with systemic ramifications: Why do systems excuse people for being afraid of Black men, assuming them to be violent? What does it mean when we as a nation permit that irrational fear of a group of people to result in repeated violence to that group, even though the fear is not actually founded in reality?

QuestLove (*aka* Ahmir Thompson) shared this in the article I mentioned earlier: "In the beginning—let's say 2002, when the gates of, 'Hey, Ahmir, would you like to come to [swanky elitist place]?' opened—I'd say 'no,' mostly because it's been hammered in my DNA to not 'rock the boat,' which means not making 'certain people' feel uncomfortable. I mean, that is a crazy way to live. Seriously, imagine a life in which you think of other people's safety and comfort first, before your own. You're programmed and taught that from the gate. It's like the opposite of entitlement."[2]

There's a lot of the experience of people of color that White people have to work really hard at relationship to get a glimpse of. And this analysis isn't how all people of color feel. But I think these things right now:

- Part of the myth of the Angry Black Man is that this particular anger is irrational and impossible to engage in a healthy way.
- Part of the myth is that anger by anyone cannot be discussed compassionately but only be confronted, because anger is an unacceptable behavior in polite society. (This is particularly true in mainline church settings, where the culture of "Midwestern nice" shapes the church in complicated ways that disallow for healthy disagreement to emerge and be addressed.)
- Part of the myth is that White people's experiences of personal frustration are the same as people of color's experiences of systemic oppression, and if White people can handle disappointments and release them, people of color shouldn't hold onto pain that has been layered on top of pain over multiple generations.

I think a lot of where this comes from is the strange stew of shame, misunderstanding, discomfort, anger, historic lack of voice, and conflict-aversion that is America and race. As a result, I don't know where to turn but Scripture in order to parse it out.

---

[2]Ahmir Thompson, "Trayvon Martin and I Ain't S---," *New York Magazine* online, July 16, 2013. Available at: http://nymag.com/daily/intelligencer/2013/07/questlove-trayvon-martin-and-i-aint-shit.html.

I had planned to reflect on the Hebrew Bible's reluctant prophets for this chapter: Jeremiah in particular springs to mind, because he doesn't jump up and down begging for the task of telling Israel that God is seriously ticked off with him. (And who can blame him? It's a lousy and humiliating road he has to travel where his own community repeatedly rejects his message.) B.K. said, "and Simon." Simon, the guy who carried the cross for Jesus? That guy? The one who gets one line in each of three gospels? He doesn't even have a speaking part.

B.K. says Simon the Cyrene captures the Black experience. With no say in the matter, he's conscripted into service with no word of thanks, "Not even from Jesus," BK says. "Well, in his defense, Jesus was a little preoccupied at the time, what with having been beaten and barely being able to walk and getting ready to get nailed to a cross," I joke a little protectively of my savior.

B.K.'s eyes light up: "And that's why it means so much to have Jesus as Lord—he understands the experience of Simon; he understands the burdens we carry because he's carried those burdens."

What B.K. is pointing to, I think, is the heart of Black Liberation Theology. It remains controversial among people who think that different ethnicities exploring theology through their own cultural lenses means that they are self-segregating when Jesus called us to be one body. (This ignores the fact that much of the theology our pastors get taught and teach us in the pews was written from a White cultural experience without ever being named explicitly, because Whiteness remains normative in our society.) Black liberation theology as it emerged in the late 1960s made the argument that Jesus is Black in that he understands the Black experience of being mistreated and maligned and pushed to the margins. Jesus knows Black people's suffering firsthand and offers freedom from that suffering in this world and not just the next, through the civil rights and Black Power movements, either with or without the church. B.K. reminded me that when he was growing up, his mostly White denomination and the mostly White National Council of Churches were on the forefront of the civil rights movement, so some of the interracial dialogue and race-related ministry in his community was funded by the NCC. He also got to work alongside the not-yet-Reverend Al Sharpton who was a close friend and high school classmate of B.K.'s brother.

There are many non-Black people of color who have been inspired by Black Liberation Theology and the doors it has opened for them to recognize the ways Jesus might understand their experiences: as a refugee to Egypt, as someone living under the colonial empire of Rome, as the child of laborers, as someone from a religion in some ways persecuted by the ruling nation, as an Indigenous person whose land was conquered. And there are White people who have found that Black liberation theology has caused them to read Scripture in a new way and recognize that they may have power and privilege of which they were not aware, seeing themselves in the Roman Centurion instead of the disciples and asking what that means for their relationship with people of color and with Jesus.

There's another theologian whom I have found really helpful in thinking about this issue of people with privilege not knowing how to engage people of color, especially those who are angry (whether justifiably or not). I got to study with a Catholic theologian named David Tracy, a kind Santa Claus–looking man who was so brilliant I usually understood about one third of what he said—on a good day. But he wrote a book called *Plurality and Ambiguity* in which he argues that part of the way people who benefit from race privilege grow deeper in their faith and relationship to Jesus is actually by preferencing voices from the margins—letting them have the floor first and more often, doing more listening and reflecting than speaking, and paying attention for where Christ's concern for the poor and marginalized makes itself clearer through their speaking and experiences. He's asking a lot of his fellow White people. And he believes the payoff is better understanding the people with whom God walks most closely: those on the margins of society. B.K. would add that the payoff is also White people understanding themselves and the impact on a world shaped by the notion of a "White race."

In my experience, the spaces where we can actually make space for anger, where we can honor other people's experiences, where we can actually look at systems that keep things the way they are even when we want them to be different—those spaces are rare, and they're just as rare in the church as everywhere else. But I met B.K. in one of those spaces. We both serve on the board of Faith Alliance for a Moral Economy, and we interact with poor people of every race, immigrant and U.S.-born, and we as faith leaders stand with them as they fight for worker justice. And we end up having hard conversations where we talk about our anger and our faith (what David Tracy refers to in another book as "Blessed Rage for Order"). And I believe we are making our corner of the world a little better in the process.

I asked B.K. whether race still matters, and he reminded me of a twenty-something woman he recently met who is "¼ Black, ¾ White." When he asked how she identified herself she claimed all identities, referencing herself as "mixed race," and he affirmed that, telling her, "Someone like you in my grandmother's generation would pass as white (Italian perhaps). Someone in my generation would have shouted, 'Say it loud; I'm Black and I'm proud.' You're being all of it. That's amazing. That's progress."

Then he continued to share with me that maybe race wasn't the driving issue today that it was for his generation. "It is true that every generation has its question. Our question was centrally engaged through the lens of race. So the question of what does it mean to be human and what is the contract we must share, that question was answered through the experience of the legacy of harm to African Americans. The civil rights movement and its successes did not happen in a vacuum; it had a meta-context. What we attribute as MLK Jr.'s success was owed in large part to the militants like Malcolm and Black Nationalists whose mantra was 'Burn Baby Burn' and 'If you kill mine, I'll kill yours,' which made nonviolent integration a much more appealing option to American power brokers. But also America was embarrassed to live out its racism in the context of Soviets saying, 'Look how they treat Blacks.' So the universal question of what it means to be a human being was answered through the lens of race in my generation."

B.K. also said: "This generation is beyond race because they're not going to talk about it or experience it in the same ways generations before did. Their question, I think, is how do we build a planet that doesn't reject us? How do we rebuild and restore a planet that has suffered the ravage of unbridled consumption and industrial poisoning? And just like my generation failed to answer our question, this generation will fail to answer that question."

I wanted to close on a more hopeful note, but this is B.K.'s story, and who's going to argue with an angry Black man?

And maybe the Beloved Community begins when we actually start listening.

CHAPTER QUESTIONS

1. Did any of the issues in this chapter surprise you? What injustices from this chapter upset you most?
2. Is there any agreement within your congregation about any injustice you could act upon?
3. What can the larger church/denomination do about any of these wrongs? Who else can they partner with to address these issues? (If you are familiar with the Moral Mondays campaign in North Carolina, what would it look like to create something like that where you live?)
4. What does it mean to your faith to look at Jesus as someone who can relate to Simon the Cyrene?
5. What does the negative experience of Black people in America have to do with the Beloved Community?

5

Perpetually Liminal

The Myth of the Perpetual Foreigner and In-Betweenness

"If it's a race,
then where is that g—d—n finish line?
I'm tired of the 'go back to where you came from!'
The 'so...how...long...have...you...been...here...in...
this...country?'
As if I ever left."

—"Race and I'm Running,"
from the spoken word group Broken Speak,
from the album "I Was Born With Two Tongues"

"So how do you deal with people putting you in a box?" I ask my Vietnamese American friend Binh[1] over a glass of wine one night.

The reason I'm asking him, I've explained, is that I want to delve into the issue of how Asian Americans are often placed in the "perpetual foreigner" role. That is, no matter how many generations we've been in the United States, or

[1]Not his real name.

how much we identify with American culture, people will ask us, "Where are you from?" and when we say, "Sandusky," or, "Burbank," they'll say, "No; where are you *really* from?"

"It's actually harder with the Vietnamese community," Binh responds.

"Wait, really?" Binh has lived in the United States since he was eight. A local church embraced him when he arrived in the United States and he became a Christian because of them. When his biological family was emotionally abusive, a White family of his high school best friend informally adopted him; when he says, "my parents," they are who he means. Binh is the most rabid Dallas Cowboys fan I know, and that's saying something. And yet, despite having lived here for over twenty years and claiming this country as inextricably his, most people look at him and see him as Asian. So his response surprises me.

"Yeah. When Americans see me, I don't have to prove myself."

"They see you as American?"

"No," he says, "they see me as Vietnamese. But the Vietnamese community—I'm always having to prove that I'm one of them."

Binh left Vietnam at four, and moved here at eight. The intervening four years were spent in a refugee camp as his family fled the communist regime in Vietnam. And those four years meant he didn't grow up learning the appropriate inflections and subtleties of language and mannerisms that many first-generation Vietnamese people (adult immigrants) or second-generation Vietnamese Americans (born on U.S. soil) would have learned in a stable setting. Binh is what Asian Americans call "the 1.5 generation," a phrase borrowed from the Korean community to describe those of us who came here between, say, ages five and fifteen, with one foot in each country, destined to translate between cultures and never be fully either one.

If I'd had this conversation with Binh eight years ago, I wonder if it might have gone differently. When I first met him, he certainly didn't deny being Asian, but it wasn't a badge of honor. As I experienced him, he seemed really interested in erasing his cultural otherness as much as possible and was more interested in people noticing his individual uniqueness and even more basically interested in people accepting him. Binh notes that it was really more of an identity crisis than it seemed; seminary demanded real clarity on where he belonged in the world.

Part of the American mythos around race is that this is exactly what we should all strive for: do not focus on what divides us culturally. Instead, celebrate what is distinctive about each of us as individuals. I won't deny something touching about that ideal, except that it is a much more attainable ideal for some of us than others. When I do anti-oppression trainings, I often do an activity with groups in which I ask them to share the things about their identities that shape how people in the world experience them. I've been doing this activity for a while now, and have learned to explain that I mean the things we have no control over. The ways that people experience me and that systems engage with me are based on these things I have no control over but give me either privilege or marginalization: my gender and gender identity; my sexual orientation; my age; my immigration status; my first language; the fact that I'm the child of two college-educated people; my class; my specific race; my developmental, emotional, and physical ability; and the religion I'm raised in. We call it an identity map, and it's designed to help reflect on the ways we sometimes don't realize we're experienced in the world based on things we might not think about a lot.

The first time I did this activity, I showed the group of pastors my own map, but I didn't explain explicitly enough that this was about things we have no control over. The people of color in the room did their maps just like I did. The White people drew maps that included, "Gardener," "Guitarist," "Baker," and "Avid Reader." They didn't include race or gender or the other details because they didn't see those things as mattering very much: No one should be judged by those things, right? So why would they write those down?

And while it made them sad that the rest of us included those things and felt we were judged by them, they had a hard time believing that people engaged them differently because their map included "White," "Straight," "Middle aged," "Married," or "Male."

When I met Binh, he looked in many ways like he was striving toward that paradigm of healthy American individualism. In reality, Binh has shared with me, it's not that he wanted to be perceived as American so much as he had very few API (Asian and Pacific Islander) friends and colleagues with whom to share his own questions of identity; his friends, his girlfriend, his faculty were almost all White. And it is possible that the handful of us who weren't White didn't create an inviting space for him to wrestle with deep questions so much as shame him for not having it all worked out already. (*Note*: Talking about feelings isn't necessarily a high priority among many of us from API immigrant communities; this is not always a good thing.)

Binh's spiritual journey has shown him that not only is it inevitable that he will be labeled Vietnamese (and so will his children—by the time this book is published, he'll be married to a Vietnamese American woman), but that there are things about his native culture that are different than the Anglo-American culture he has adopted. He celebrates both cultures and in many ways is quintessentially American, but in some ways it is more troubling to have to prove his Vietnamese status to the (particularly first-generation) Vietnamese community here that expects mastery of certain unwritten rules that he was never taught. In the past, if one Vietnamese church or club didn't accept him, he could shrug his shoulders and try the next one, but as he marries into a Vietnamese family, he will not have that option.

A lot of people find it hard to see what's so bad about being the "Model Minority." In fact, some Asian Americans embrace that idea, or they believe that they are functionally White. Binh knows different. He doesn't pretend not to notice that he'll never really be considered White, and he knows that people will unconsciously impose an identity on him, not just of being good at math and a hard worker, but also of not being capable of creativity or leadership. He also doesn't see White as a thing to aspire to, which is the very subtle agenda of racism: making White normative and aspirational (and also something people of color can't actually attain). He also rejects the model minority myth because he does not want to participate in the ways Asian immigrants are used as a lever in systems of racism that preserve White power and privilege at the expense of Black people.[2]

Binh has chosen to accept that his adoptive country will put him into a box. He is not ready to accept that his own biological community does not assign him the same box. And as his fiancé's family tentatively adopts him, the pain of not being taken at face value simply as Binh is something he must face daily. Binh, in many ways, defines liminality even as he seeks to defy it.

> **Liminal:** (1): of or relating to a sensory threshold; (2): barely perceptible; (3): of, relating to, or being an intermediate state, phase, or condition: in between; transitional (Merriam-Webster Dictionary).

I find myself thinking about the book of Ruth. Ruth doesn't start out as liminal, and the text isn't explicit that she is, but the story of Ruth starts at home and ends up in between. Ruth is a Moabite who is married to an Israelite in her homeland of Moab. When her husband dies, her mother-in-law Naomi tells her Ruth will have better luck staying in Moab than following Naomi back to Judah. (Widows had it hard no matter what. Immigrant widows were unlikely to get *any* support, which was why Naomi was uprooting herself with both her husband and sons dead in a foreign land.) While Naomi's other widowed daughter-in-law, Orpah, takes Naomi's sage advice and stays in her homeland, Ruth

---

[2]For example, in the fall of 2014, White anti-affirmative action activist Edward Blum brought together some Asian Americans rejected by elite universities, alleging an anti-Asian bias. (Blum went to the Supreme Court in 2012 arguing the same bias against a White woman.) This is despite the fact that 65% of Asian Americans support affirmative action. An API counter-movement refers to itself online as #IAmNotYourWedge.

demurs. You know the moving Scripture in which Ruth promises not to leave Naomi (popular in lesbian weddings due to some scholars' belief that Ruth and Naomi had romantic love for one another; I also think it is a powerful wedding vow for mixed-race couples to speak to each other, both claiming each other's culture):

> "Where you go I will go, and where you stay I will stay. Your people will be my people and your God my God. Where you die I will die, and there I will be buried. May the LORD deal with me, be it ever so severely, if even death separates you and me." (Ruth 1:16b–17, NIV)

I find myself thinking about it because the average reader 2,000 years ago would have understood that Ruth had to do some self-sacrificing, potentially self-debasing things in order to survive in her adoptive land of Judah. She loved Naomi enough to do them, but that didn't make them less self-sacrificial. The prime example is sleeping with the very old Boaz so he will have to marry her and take care of Naomi as well—options for survival available to women at the time were incredibly limited.

I also find myself thinking that, according to author Aaron Taylor, Boaz was directly contradicting Jewish teachings in Nehemiah by marrying a Moabite.[3] I suspect life was difficult for Ruth in Judah, even if she ended up being great-grandmother to King David. I suspect that, while the text says the people of Judah celebrate her faithfulness and loyalty to Naomi, she still faced slights and disrespect as a Jew-by-choice as opposed to a biological inheritor of the faith.

For many people, the book of Ruth is a beautiful story of one woman's deep devotion to another and her willingness to do whatever is asked of her for the sake of that other woman (whether the relation is filial or otherwise). And many people add the layer of her devotion to God, which they infer from her devotion to Naomi and then to Boaz, and from the people

---

[3]Access this essay at: http://sojo.net/blogs/2010/05/25/further-reflections-biblical-ruth-illegal-immigrant.

of Judah believing that her fertility shows God's favor upon her. An immigrant might notice the parts of the story that get left out. The Hebrew Bible is explicit about treating the foreigner well and remembering that "we were foreigners in Egypt." And yet, it is equally clear about the need to distrust and not intermarry with people of other tribes. An adoptive child of the one true God is caught between the ideal of Scripture and the reality of people's suspicion of the "other." An immigrant might notice that the same thing is true in America today—the tension between "all [people] are created equal" and racial profiling or simply, "Where are you from?"

Binh and I are both Americans by choice. We're also both Christians by choice. And not being Americans from birth or Christians from birth means we're sometimes viewed as a little suspect within those categories. I usually tell people my cultural heritage before they ask, because I know the puzzle that is the combination of my Indian name and my light olive skin and my red hair. (It's henna, and Indians have been dying their hair with it for hundreds of years. Going gray at age 14 is its own burden.) I tell them so they can puzzle out the box I fit in. And, I promise, they get frustrated when I don't stay in that box, even if different people assign me to different boxes.

I experienced a moment of hope recently in regard to what it means to be liminal. During the biggest of the protests for justice in Ferguson in October 2014, the organization 18 Million Rising marched prominently. 18MR advocates for Asian and Pacific Islander rights, but it does not aspire to becoming acceptable to White people or to becoming an isolated API community that only cares about its own rights. The reason this matters so much to me is that Asian Americans are taught in subtle ways that aligning ourselves with Black people is against our self-interest if we want to get by in the United States; as a result, we get co-opted into the culture of anti-Blackness illustrated in the previous chapter. We're taught that to avoid generations of liminality we need to distance ourselves from the Black struggle; or we're taught to distance ourselves from it lest we suffer worse than liminality. In contrast, 18MR stood there in Ferguson on behalf of Binh and me and said, "Black Lives Matter to the API Community. Caring about other people on the margins, in the liminal spaces, is what it means to be us."[4]

I think that action matters so much to me because as a kid who was incredibly liminal throughout elementary school, my first moment of feeling not completely alone in the world was when my fourth grade class studied Martin Luther King Jr. He piqued my interest because he was influenced by Mahatma Gandhi, and I remained proud of the fact that my father had taken my mother and me to see the movie *Gandhi* when I was in first grade and I got to see a three-hour movie that started at 8 p.m., so I knew our legacies were connected. I read every book in our school library about Dr. King, who had said everyone should be treated equal and named the fact that, in America, not everyone *was* treated equal. I even made my music teacher play the sheet music from "We Shall Overcome" after class because I had never heard it before. Dr. King was my first teacher that my experience of liminality wasn't just that I was weird; it was that the country wrapped around me was weird. I'm glad to finally be at a point in my life when I get to respond to that teaching in solidarity with those for whom Dr. King most stood. I'm glad I have API allies like 18MR and Binh to teach me how to do that well.

I'm not sure whether my children will be asked, "Where are you from? No, where are you *really* from?" the way that I know Binh's children will. And I hope that our respective children will in fact be recognized for being gardeners and musicians and mathematicians even more than for their cultural identity. And I dream of a Beloved Community in which they will feel embraced by a cultural community that is open to their way of being Asian even if it is not identical to "how it was done in the old country."

---

[4]After the December 2014 non-indictment in the death of Eric Garner, an informal Asian American group gathered to make public our solidarity, and to direct it toward other Asian Americans. You can find the video project at http://dearasians.tumblr.com.

But I suspect that for at least another generation, they will be liminal: not fully one or fully the other. Not Naomi, and not Orpah. To some they will be strangers in a strange land, even if that land is the only one they really know. To others, they will be too contaminated by this strange land to truly belong to the homeland. They will have the choice not to be hurt by fitting in neither box. But they will have to accept that the boxes still exist, even when people keep insisting that the boxes went away generations ago.

CHAPTER QUESTIONS

1. Have you had experiences of not fitting in? How did you find yourself relating or not relating to Binh's story?
2. If you have children, how are they defined by the people around them? (Like or unlike how Binh's children will always be seen as not fully American.) How does that make you feel?
3. Do you read the story of Ruth differently in thinking of her as a foreigner dealing with the challenges that foreigners often face? If so, how? Can you relate to her more or less?
4. What does the concept of liminality have to do with the Beloved Community?

6

Isn't It Really about Class?

"Both class and race survive education, and neither should. What is education then? If it doesn't help a human being to recognize that humanity is humanity, what is it for? So you can make a bigger salary than other people?"

—Beah Richards

Two of my favorite people in Oakland are conscious hip hop artist LaDasha "Diamond" Berry and Poverty Skola Lisa "Tiny" Garcia.[1] They both grew up poor; they were both raised by strong Black women; they're both raising sons they love deeply; and they both chose to stay in their communities to strengthen them.

I wish you could see them. LaDasha is a glorious full-figured chocolate-skinned woman with long black hair with light highlights who always looks classier than me in her form-fitting slacks or skirt and top. Lisa is a petite, light-skinned woman; you can usually see her long, straight blonde-streaked hair under her almost permanently affixed

[1]"Conscious hip hop" is a designation for the sub-genre of hip hop that addresses social and social justice concerns, as opposed to other styles of hip hop. A not-perfect analogy would be "conscious hip hop is to hip hop what protest songs are to folk music." Not all hip hop artists who take on social issues would self-identify as conscious hip hop artists, but some do.

baseball cap. For two powerful women from the same community and dedicated to the same community, they could not look more different.

That's why I wanted to talk with them about the question I get asked more than any other when I facilitate anti-racism workshops (with the hint of a suggestion that I am distracting the group from the important work of the day): "Really? You think we need to talk about race? Isn't it really about class? Isn't that the real issue that is dividing America?"

Usually the question comes from middle-class White people, which isn't a reason to dismiss it, but I do find myself suspecting that this is a way to avoid an uncomfortable issue I'm raising—the issue of White privilege (addressed in a previous chapter). At the same time, I do occasionally hear the same issue raised by poor people of color, and it's a question I have actually asked myself with some small amount of guilt. *What if it really is more about class, and I'm beating a dead horse, while not sufficiently addressing an issue that is killing people?*

Lisa works with a grassroots nonprofit organization called POOR Magazine: Prensa POBRE. It has a reputation for being progressive, cutting edge, radical, and revolutionary. (These words are used as compliments and insults depending on who's saying them.) POOR works on a landless people's movement they call "homefulness" in deep east Oakland. She notes that in their research, they've discovered that there is a particular point at which race does not matter: when you are part of the street community (the community of people who do not have homes), specifically if you fit the "Western Euro-centric therapy complex" definition of "mentally ill," by which Lisa means that people on the street experience equal discrimination regardless of race if they do not behave in socially sanctioned ways (if they behave in ways some people would describe as "crazy"). Age and physical ability also factor into how members of the street community are treated by passersby and also by law enforcement and the people who call on them. Homeless people experience the same levels of disruption and harassment by law enforcement regardless of race. At POOR Magazine, Lisa comments,

"Poppa Bear is our panhandler reporter; he's already dealing with sit/lie,[2] which you deal with no matter what color you are," she comments, then jokes, "which is a beautiful democratizing process." However, even then, race shows up: "He's also been visited by homeland security because his [given] name sounds like a terrorist."

The Oakland Peace Center, where I work, hosted a showing of POOR Magazine's poverty skolaz-written play "Hotel Voices," about life in SROs in San Francisco. SROs, or Single Resident Occupancy hotels, are low-cost apartments that can usually be rented by the week and are notoriously poor in quality, since poor people have so few housing options in the most expensive city in the nation. Lisa played the part of the narrator: a bedbug. Lisa knows firsthand the complex interweaving of race and poverty from her own upbringing in the SROs of San Francisco. When she and her mom were living in their car and needed to get inside, her dark-skinned mother would walk into an SRO "and immediately get turned down as a poor woman of color with no credit," says Lisa. "I would put on a suit we got at Kmart and when I was twelve I'd go in looking white pretending I was twenty-five and earning $65k and we'd get a place. That's a strategy for survival," she explains.

LaDasha likewise sees race and class as both mattering: "A lot of the time people get judged based off of physical appearance before what's in their hearts or bank accounts. That's the history of America and that's always been a factor." LaDasha and I had been talking about Oprah not being allowed into a fancy store in Paris because all they saw was a Black woman, even though she's one of the richest people in the world. LaDasha commented, "People keep trying to take race out of the equation, but what about people of color who have money and still get treated wrong? How can you

[2]"Sit/Lie" is the abbreviation of an ordinance gaining popularity in cities across the country as a way of making illegal the act of sitting or lying down in public places, including sidewalks. Critics point out that such laws are enforced selectively, targeting homeless people. (Poppa Bear passed away prior to the publishing of this book.)

enslave people and then expect that to be forgotten? It was even in our laws. How are we going to forget that without addressing it head on?"

I describe LaDasha as a conscious hip hop artist, but she notes that she's caught between conscious hip hop and gangsta rap, "because of everything I saw coming up on Seminary." Seminary Avenue is in east Oakland, and in the fall of 2013 a popular local hip hop artist, Kafani, was shot and paralyzed during a video shoot there. Gangsta rap names the lived realities of the street while conscious hip hop names the community we aspire to—it's positive, it's life-affirming, and it's supposed to be fun. I actually had LaDasha perform one of her songs when I pastored First Christian Church of Oakland: "Do Something" was the refrain, and it invited the congregation and the community to be the change we wish to see in the world. She and her sons also performed it at the launch of the Oakland Peace Center.

LaDasha has recently landed a job working with children in Oakland public schools, which is a dream come true for someone dedicated to strengthening the next generation of children. LaDasha attributes her sense of values and commitment to giving back to being raised by her grandmother after LaDasha's mother was shot when LaDasha was two. While she celebrates the mature values her grandmother passed on to her, LaDasha didn't stay out of trouble completely. Coming up in her neighborhood, she faced one of the tricky aspects of the intersection of race and class: "I was good at school, which made things hard. Kids would fight me for being too smart." Eventually her grandmother sent her to live in a suburb with her aunt and uncle instead, where there were more accepted ways of being a person of color, and where everyone was encouraged to be their best selves, including LaDasha.

This theme has come up in a few different ways in a few different chapters, so here's a brief summary of my thoughts on this issue of class and race. It is really hard to grow up poor and White in America. There are lots of barriers to success. At the same time, there are many stories for what it means to be White—being White in America doesn't have one fixed narrative, so if you are smart or you're a good dancer or you're a poet or you're a chef or you excel at sports, those are all acceptable ways of being White. The narrative of what it means to be a person of color is much more constrained (again, the danger of the single story), and White people aren't the only ones who learn those constrained narratives—people of color internalize those constrained narratives, too. And we impose those narratives on each other within our communities. However, poverty has its own culture, and people are definitely judged and judge themselves based on that culture as well.

I previously defined racism as race privilege plus misuse of power by systems and institutions. Classism looks about the same to me: class privilege plus misuse of power by systems and institutions. I benefit a lot from class privilege. And it intersects with race in lots of messy ways. Another definition we might use is the following: "Classism is prejudice or discrimination on the basis of social class. It includes individual attitudes and behaviors, systems of policies and practices that are set up to benefit the upper classes at the expense of the lower classes."[3]

I benefit a lot from class privilege: I grew up without debt shaping my decisions. I grew up knowing where my next meal would come from and with access to healthy and nutritious food. I grew up with a sense that the criminal justice system would be fair in the way it dealt with me. I grew up with access to culture and with enough resources to experience it occasionally. While I am currently considered "very low income" by the standards of the region I live in, I know that if I lost my job, I would have a safety net of friends and family so I would not go homeless or without food; I probably wouldn't even lose my home. And if I gave up my particular calling, I could probably earn more money than I currently do—I have the option of doing what I want to do

---

[3]For *Wikipedia's* definition of classism, see: http://en.wikipedia.org/wiki/Class_privilege.

for a living, which my parents did not have because their choices were dictated by their financial obligations. Because I grew up middle class, I know how to access resources when I do get into a hard spot. Like most people of color who live in multiple contexts at the same time, I can "code switch" in order to be understood in different settings, but I was raised pretty fluent in White middle class communication style.

Both Lisa and LaDasha talk about "code switching," the term used for being able to switch between your community's colloquial language and culture and into the dominant language and culture. Some see it as a survival technique for people in marginalized communities, and some see it as an indicator of what is unhealthy in American society—that only one language and culture really gives a person access to resources. LaDasha came up in a poor community but was raised by a grandmother who took her to church and taught her to read using the *King James Bible*: "I learned how to code switch by growing up with Grandma and reading the Bible in church. When I got to ninth grade and read Shakespeare, it was easy." Combine that with genes from a free-spirited radical father and LaDasha was born to be an advocate for young women's empowerment and a wordsmith of hip hop—LaDasha learned how to use the language that would give her access to college and then stayed in her community to nurture and strengthen the next generation of women who knew the same hardships and discrimination she did.

Lisa approaches the issue of code switching from a slightly different vantage point, although with the same goal in mind. "Poor folks have our own culture on top of the other cultures we come from; we come from the Poor Nation and our ways of being are most definitely different. Those cultural signifiers play in ways we are silenced, left out, and kept out." While Lisa knows that there is a way of code switching that can give some of her community access to better financial resources, "When you code switch out of poverty, you also code switch out of culture." We usually lose a deep connection with the people who shaped us and with our ancestors in the process, and there are not enough resources to fill that void; to code switch and stay in that other language and culture damages both the people who make the switch and the community left behind, says Lisa.

The question of code switching addresses several topics already named in this book. Several of the people I interviewed came up from poverty and ended up well educated and slightly better resourced. They remain committed to the wellbeing of their communities, but tensions sit there between them and their immediate family. African American friends who have called or been called "bourgie," a Black-specific derogatory term for "bourgeois," know what I'm talking about. In my own family, my father kind of jokes (although he's not *really* joking) about how I need the best everything. I may eat organic because I'm against the chemicals farm workers are exposed to and buy fair trade to end child slavery, but for a family that bought what was on sale and lived frugally so our money could go back to the family in India, I'm just the South Asian version of bourgie.

In addition, along with poverty and racism, we often internalize that "single story." We often internalize the messages we receive about ourselves. As a result, when someone claims the space of who they are and it doesn't fit with the script, we within poor or people of color communities can feel like the other person is trying to remove themselves from our community—which is part of why LaDasha got beaten up in school; some of her classmates had internalized the message that thriving academically was a White trait, and if LaDasha was good in school, she must not want to claim her community.

A real struggle in this intersection of class and race is the cost of accessing privilege or resources. This is true for poor White people and for people of color, both of whom struggle with the barriers to greater resources. Also, for those who access those resources, there can be a cost: losing a connection with their community or their culture or the values they held dear that are not the values in their new community.

My lived experience is as a middle class immigrant of color. When I started high school, my family moved to a rich community despite being solidly middle class. We were the only non-White family living in that community, and my father kept demanding realtors show us that neighborhood instead of the more predominantly Asian and South Asian community they kept steering us toward. We made our neighbors uncomfortable because when we invited them over to dinner, we were busy in the kitchen preparing the meal, while they hired staff to cater dinners so they could be present with their guests in the living room until the meal was ready. What we saw as the gift of our labor they saw as being rude hosts. Along with that value came appearances mattering more than substance and isolation from one another—our neighbors were not the people we'd call if we were in crisis. We soon learned that our values weren't in sync with those of our community. As soon as I graduated from high school, my parents moved back to the more rural middle class community we had initially immigrated to, which shared values more in sync with theirs. "Moving on Up," as the song goes—the "American Dream"—would have cost my parents too much of their understanding of themselves and what mattered to them.

I find myself often thinking about Martin Luther King's famous sermon, "The Drum Major Instinct," about his interaction with his White jailers:

> The other day I was saying, I always try to do a little converting when I'm in jail. And when we were in jail in Birmingham the other day, the white wardens and all enjoyed coming around the cell to talk about the race problem. And they were showing us where we were so wrong demonstrating. And they were showing us where segregation was so right. And they were showing us where intermarriage was so wrong. So I would get to preaching, and we would get to talking—calmly, because they wanted to talk about it. And then we got down one day to the point—that was the second or third day—to talk about where they lived, and how much they were earning. And when those brothers told me what

> they were earning, I said, "Now, you know what? You ought to be marching with us. [*laughter*] You're just as poor as Negroes." And I said, "You are put in the position of supporting your oppressor, because through prejudice and blindness, you fail to see that the same forces that oppress Negroes in American society oppress poor white people. And all you are living on is the satisfaction of your skin being white, and the drum major instinct of thinking that you are somebody big because you are white. And you're so poor you can't send your children to school. You ought to be out here marching with every one of us every time we have a march."
>
> Now that's a fact. That the poor white has been put into this position, where through blindness and prejudice, he is forced to support his oppressors. And the only thing he has going for him is the false feeling that he's superior because his skin is white—and can't hardly eat and make his ends meet week in and week out.[4]

As I've mentioned before, Dr. King is a real hero of mine, spiritually and prophetically. And while he gave this sermon in 1968, it hints at some of the complexity that keeps both race and class issues in America trapped in amber. We get taught distrust of one another, and we get taught in very subtle ways about our inferiority or superiority. And we get taught historical amnesia: "My ancestors didn't own slaves, so I don't benefit from White privilege," for example. So we are unable to be in deeper solidarity with one another.

It probably goes without saying, but class plays a huge role in keeping people divided. The "99 Percent" slogan of the Occupy Wall Street movement may have been overly simplistic, but it reminded me that my own marginal class privilege came at a huge cost: it kept me out of relationship with poor people, when we actually shared the experience of

---

[4]Text of speech is available through stanford.edu's collection of Martin Luther King Jr. papers: http://mlk-kpp01.stanford.edu/index.php/encyclopedia/documentsentry/doc_the_drum_major_instinct/ .

being a part of a system that undervalued the work of poor people and lined the pockets of a handful of people who had no accountability to any of us. All of this is what has me thinking about Jesus and the woman at the well in the gospel of John, chapter 4.

The woman is a Samaritan, considered polluted and inferior by the Jewish community at the time. She comes to the well at midday, suggesting she may have been shunned by the other women, who would go to the well early in the morning or late in the evening instead of in the heat of the sun. Jesus probably shouldn't have been talking to a woman at all, far less a Samaritan woman.

Theologian David Lose points out that we commonly assume that she has loose morals, as a woman with five husbands over the course of her life—including a current husband who is not really her husband. Lose clarifies that we make that assumption without any indication that this is true from the text. Jesus never calls her to repentance, nor does she repent; he simply shows her that he sees her and knows her narrative, which may involve heartbreak and loss and possibly being in a loveless and dependent situation of being cared for by her dead husband's brother, known as a "levirate marriage."[5]

Jesus chooses to engage her with dignity and affirmation and solidarity, offering the living water of eternal life to her and her community, sending her forth to be one of the first evangelists. Our faith is rooted in a savior who chooses to call leaders who were poor, marginalized, and considered inferior on multiple fronts. He reaches across cultural divides despite not being a wealthy man himself. He invites his disciples to check their false notions of superiority at the door since everyone in the region shares an experience of hard living under the Roman Empire (the 1 percent). He even speaks with compassion to Roman prison guards, calling them into being their better selves.

---

[5]David Lose, "Misogyny, Morality and the Woman at the Well," *Huffington Post*, March 21, 2011. Available at: http://www.huffingtonpost.com/david-lose/misogyny-moralism-and-the_b_836753.html.

I see reflections of this way of being in LaDasha and Lisa, in the face of this challenging intersection of race and class in which they dwell and which they strive to address.

LaDasha and I talk about the shootings in Oakland, people we know, or friends of friends. We talk about how many of the shootings (often by and of Black people) are over small things, particularly about escalating issues of feeling disrespected by one another. LaDasha names a deep issue: "It's straight up Willie Lynch," she says, referring to a famous address by a slave owner who explained that the way to keep slaves in check was to pit them against each other. "That's our job; to help the people we work with look at what's going on and ask, 'Do you know why you do that?'" LaDasha works to help poor people of color in her community recognize their innate value and the value of the people she works with. This is a clear but simple way she addresses the intersection of race and class, both of which shape her community. It is a clear but simple way she also builds up a community of Women at the Well, evangelizing for peace based on their recognition of their value and others' value.

Lisa also names the way we can be hurt by our lack of understanding that the Willie Lynch culture hurts all of us, quoting her mother: "As Mama Dee would say, 'White culture isn't good for anybody, including white people.'" As discussed previously, this isn't to say White people bring bad cultures, and, in fact, each distinct culture—Welsh, Irish, Italian, and so forth—can offer great riches to our understandings of our history and our present. However, the culture that has been created by America to divide poor White people from poor people of color, the culture that creates privilege for some at the expense of equality for others, *that* culture hurts everyone, including the people it is supposed to lift up.

Lisa and POOR Magazine take on the same issue Dr. King takes on in his Drum Major Instinct sermon: "The key piece for us of organizing with communities of color, indigenous people of color, and poor white people and elders and young people and disabled peoples is to articulate each struggle to give each its own life and dignity, to not try to take it out of its trauma, its pain, and its value. It's not that people's differences need to stop or need to change. It's just that we need to actually honor and love them all. Therein lies the thing that takes more time and more energy." As a result, a major slogan within POOR Magazine is, "The Revolution will not be melted in a pot or sewn in a quilt."[6] As part of our growth into solidarity with one another, another slogan within POOR that reminds us all of what we're growing toward is this: "The Revolution Begins with 'I' and then becomes 'We.'" What I bring to the table may be the experience of being Asian American. What you bring may be the experience of poverty. What someone else brings may be about gender or orientation. We don't have to fight over which issue is the one that matters. We start from where we are and move into ally-ship with one another.

I am grateful to have LaDasha and Lisa in my life to remind me of what it means to be conscious of both race *and* class instead of thinking I have to address one or the other. My experience as a middle class immigrant person of color is a story of both privilege and marginalization, and I can know myself, and my role in the work of reconciliation, when I acknowledge that whole story and hear others' whole stories.

When "I" becomes "we," when Samaritan women can guide and lead Roman centurions to a better collective way of living, when I can recognize my worth and also yours, we are a little closer to breaking down the barriers of racism and classism, and we grow a little closer to the Beloved Community.

---

[6]The "melting pot" metaphor for America can be problematic in that it erases our individual cultural identities. Many foundations that fund nonprofit work have therefore started using the image of a tapestry that is woven together of all of our distinct cultures. Lisa is perhaps cautioning us that our distinct contributions still get lost in that tapestry, and we are only useful insofar as we fit into a project created for us: a tapestry. If we don't fit into the frame (if our color stands out too much), we are not valuable to the project.

CHAPTER QUESTIONS

1. Do you judge people by their clothing, vocabulary, or accent?
2. Are there similarities between class bias and race bias? How do you see them show up similarly or differently? Is there a double penalty for some members of the community who are seen as both?
3. What parts of LaDasha's story resonate for you? What parts of Lisa's? What parts are different than your own story?
4. Do you think that race does divide poor White people and poor people of color, as Dr. King suggested? Do you think the divisions between Samaritans and Jews helped Roman authorities retain power in the region?
5. What does talking about race as well as class have to do with the Beloved Community?

7

Race and Religion Post 9/11

"There has been a tendency to view the post-9/11 backlash only in the distant past. In the year after 9/11, anti-Muslim hate crimes rose by nearly 1,600%. Although these numbers have not been as high over the past 11 years, bias incidents continue to be reported and the climate of prejudice has arguably become worse. It manifests itself in different ways: a mosque blocked for the past two years from being developed in Tennessee; a Bangladeshi cab driver brutally assaulted in New York because his passenger thought he was Muslim; and a mosque in Missouri destroyed by a suspected arson a day after the Oak Creek tragedy. It extends to politicians, such as Rep. Peter King, R-N.Y., holding anti-Muslim hearings and Rep. Michele Bachmann, R-Minn., making unsubstantiated claims that disloyal Muslims are infiltrating our government."

—Deepa Iyer[1]

As I've mentioned before, I used to work for an interfaith organization that advocated for religious liberty. It was a good cause and the people I worked with were like a second family.

---

[1]Deepa Iyer, "Post-9/11 discrimination must end," USA Today, September 8, 2012. Available at: http://usatoday30.usatoday.com/news/opinion/forum/story/2012-08-09/sikh-shooting-muslims-bias/56920502/1.

But, in my twenties, I didn't really think the work was quite as hardcore as I would like. I wanted to be part of a movement for justice like they had in the Sixties. I understood that in some parts of the country, people tried to impose one religion (Christianity) and diminish the value of others, and that was an important issue to address, but not "Resurgence of the Klan" important. Not "Black Churches Burning" important. (Both of these things were happening in the late 1990s.) I kept nudging the organization to get more deeply immersed in racial justice issues, which seemed to me to affect so many more people so much more severely.

I left the organization in August of 2001 to take a month off before starting seminary. About a month later, my slightly self-righteous attitude about the issue of civil rights being a different category from religious freedom got pretty well shredded.

South Asians[2] have different narratives of our experience in the wake of 9/11. Many of us were here for economic advancement, and South Asians were the most upwardly mobile of all Asian immigrant groups. (A well-kept secret in America is that not all Asian and Pacific Islander communities thrive at the same rate, and the API community faces issues of poverty and discrimination and language barriers even despite the "model minority myth" that hides and creates deeper shame around experiences of poverty among API people.) Some of us clung to the idea that nothing had changed—we were still American; this was about a small subset and had nothing to do with us. Even in the face of horrible experiences of violence against Muslims, some of us remained stalwart that this was an issue of religion, not race.

I was staying with my parents in Akron when 9/11 happened. A mosque in Cleveland was firebombed on the following Friday night. My father had to go to a bank in

[2]I use the term "South Asian" instead of "Indian" or "east Indian" because, in America, people from Pakistan, Bangladesh, Sri Lanka, Afghanistan, and India are generally lumped together. Some first-generation immigrants claim their particular national affiliation. However, many second-generation immigrants recognize that we do have a shared experience in America worth claiming. This became even more apparent to many of us after 9/11.

Cleveland on Saturday morning to make a deposit. "Please don't," I begged. "It's not safe." My father's brown skin, I was certain, made him a target.

"Oh, I will make a T-shirt that says, 'I am Hindu. We hate Muslims, too!'" he joked and laughed.

My father grew up in a half-Muslim, half-Hindu village in India. He's markedly less prejudiced towards Muslims than my cousins my own age who have grown up in post-partition India, which has deepened and cultivated divisions and hostilities along religious lines. If you know him, you know he would never do that.

But after 9/11, when race and religion blurred, that's exactly what happened in parts the South Asian community.

Some of us read the stories about attacks on Sikhs increasing by 1,000 percent after 9/11 and realized the South Asian American community needed to be in solidarity with itself and with other targeted groups. The backlash was growing, and the targets were becoming increasingly indiscriminate. Being brown became a liability. Some of us read stories about Mexican Americans being beaten up in the Southwest for "looking Arab" and began to realize that racism was inspiring lethal and deadly violence.

Some of us were actually reflective enough to realize that the firebombing of a mosque was dangerous. Some of us recognized that the destruction was a form of religious intimidation of an entire faith group—tarred by the actions of gang of extreme outliers claiming allegiance to a tradition with a billion adherents across the globe. As the public dialogue led by our President adopted apocryphal imagery of good and evil, some us began to use an analogy that was more accurate: Muslim is to Terrorist as Christian is to KKK.

But some of us did not see things this way. Instead, driven by fear and the awareness that we might not be able to retain our relatively high spot in the ever-shifting racial hierarchy of the United States, we began drawing bright lines. Some of us felt comfortable suggesting that not all of us were real Americans and that faith association was the clear test. That is, some of us were ready to throw Muslims under the bus.

Shortly after 9/11 a group of South Asian community leaders convened out of concern about the growing backlash, particularly acts of violence targeting observant Sikh men wearing turbans and ethnic garb.[3] At one of the early meetings, a group of fifteen met to discuss strategies for challenging the wave of hate and began to think about what they could do as a group to shift the conversation to that of healing.

In that meeting was a friend of mine, Layla.[4] She is a Muslim woman who does not wear a hijab or cover in a traditional outer garment or burka. Her experience in interfaith settings began early, as her parents moved often between small cities across the Midwest. Blending in was second nature for Layla; it was a survival instinct borne out of the experience of being the only Muslim and, often, only non-White person in the parochial school classes she attended growing up. She was also an activist and had worked as an organizer.

Layla blended in so naturally as one of the group that others in the circle did not realize she was Muslim. When the question was raised, "How can we quickly bring an end to the senseless violence and wave of hate and frenzied targeting of observant Sikhs?" the suggestions stunned her: "We should print red, white, and blue t-shirts that say, 'We're Sikhs, a peace loving people, not Muslim Terrorists,' and wear flag-printed turbans."

Suddenly she realized that this room full of other South Asians who represented a mix of secular, Hindu, and Sikh men and women of different generations didn't know she

---

[3]Many Americans in this moment did not realize that Sikhs, whose religion requires the men to wear a turban, are a different religion from Muslims, probably because Osama Bin Laden, a Muslim, happened to wear a turban. It goes without saying that people shouldn't have been harming Muslims who had nothing to do with the attack on the Twin Towers, but they were also often attacking people from a completely different religion than the one they were misguidedly intending to attack.

[4]Not her real name.

was Muslim and clearly saw Muslim as "a threat," maybe to their safety but particularly to their reputation: they did not want to be damned by association. Not only was she blending in a little too well, but her assumption that they felt a sense of "community" may have been premature. She wasn't naïve. Layla knew that anti-Muslim and anti-Hindu biases existed, but assumed community leaders trying to address hate crimes functioned on a higher plane.

After all, she shared with me later, "You don't slip off your shoes, cross your legs, and find a seat on the floor to begin brainstorming on best ways to heal your community if you are bigoted toward Muslims, right?"

But then again, history and sociology remind us that intragroup bias is a time-honored experience of new immigrant groups in the United States.

The social hierarchy of privilege tests every ethnic group that arrives on our shores. From the stories of Irish versus Italian at the turn-of-the-twentieth-century Boston and New York to the tensions between Jews and Catholics, the story is the same.

When you arrive on American shores, you are asked in a million subtle ways: Do you find solidarity with the excluded "others," or do you work to shed distinctions and convince people with power that you are one of them? How far you are from the top of the hierarchy is often tested by your group attitudes and views of others closer to the bottom. In fact, distinguishing your group from the bottom is almost a pastime in South Asian communities. Echoing and adopting the dominant negative attitudes and biases harbored toward the most socially excluded is seen to demonstrate allegiance to those at the top of the privilege chain. And since most South Asians come to this country speaking English and connected to family who entered due to high-level skills, our position in the racial hierarchy was such that many South Asians were blindsided by the vitriol that seemed to emerge from nowhere (even if it emerged from a long narrative of race in the country with which South Asians were mostly ill acquainted).

Layla should not have been totally surprised, but she was deeply disappointed.

I've known Layla for many years now. She and I traded numerous stories before 9/11 about what it's like to be part of the third race culture in America: neither Black nor White, and also connected to the non-Judeo Christian world. Layla is Muslim and my father is Hindu; most Christians have no idea how heavily shaped by Christianity America is in ways that are often diminishing of and sometimes dangerous to non-Christians.

Translating her faith and finding a space (as neither White nor Black) offered its challenges as Layla grew up in the American Midwest and South. A couple months after being enrolled in a predominantly White kindergarten, she decided one day to stop speaking. "At school the kids laughed at me because I was pronouncing and using words incorrectly and at home I was not allowed to speak English even though my broken Urdu drew near-constant corrections. At no point could I say something without interruption. I was five years old and I was angry and felt like my literal voice was being silenced so I decided that I was done speaking!"

Caught between two tongues, she decided to use neither in an early form of what she nostalgically refers to as her first act of civil disobedience. Her parents and teachers, first frustrated then concerned that she was exhibiting either a learning disability or emotional problems finally got her to break the self-imposed silence by giving her permission to speak wherever and however she wanted. (Ironically, now you can't get her to stop speaking, and we're better for it.)

As she entered adolescence, her parents did not ask her to cover her hair but insisted on her practicing the Muslim value of modesty. As Layla began to express her Muslim identity as a young teen, she found herself once again caught between two worlds when she moved to the American South. During her last year in junior high she found herself in a vastly different world from the all-White parochial schools of the rural Midwest. She attended a predominantly African American junior high school, with 99 percent urban African American students and less than 1 percent Whites. Layla and her sibling were the only non-White, non-Black students in the school.

During eighth grade she found her clothing became a source of constant scrutiny: "Why aren't you wearing shorts?" "Why do your shirts go past your butt?"

She didn't explain the pants in gym class were about the culture of modesty in her religion. She guessed eighth graders probably wouldn't be compassionate about yet another thing that made her not like them. One day the scrutiny ended: "Six weeks into school, on gym day I braced for the fight that was coming. I was in the locker room and mentally preparing to get shoved. The accusations started along with the pokes as we changed. It always started with, 'Oh, you think you're special because you are so light skinned and your hair is straight,' and then rapidly devolved with laser focus onto my baggy pants and long shirts. But Yolanda, my "bully" by today's definition, noticed my fumbling attempts to change pants without revealing my undergarments. She declared, 'Your butt is so small and you're embarrassed, right?!' This was her confident declaration and it made sense to the locker room full of preening girls half-dressed competing for mirror time. My first instinct was to laugh, but then I realized that would result in a confrontation. If I went along, she and the others might show some pity and I would not have to explain."

Such are the compromises people who live between cultures make to get through the day, especially in junior high. As a teenager, Layla worked with youth in understanding race, religion, and immigration issues. She volunteered for human relations workshops and became a teen trainer for the National Conference of Christians and Jews chapter in her city. All this interest in race and identity and religion began in the South, sparked literally by being caught between two boxes on a traffic citation: "I was sixteen and driving 10 miles over the speed limit when I was pulled over by an African American police officer. When I reviewed the ticket she handed me I politely refused to sign it because the violation did not describe me. It denoted my race as White. I said that I could not sign a document that is false and I promised to challenge it if she forced me to take it. Left with only one of two boxes to choose, she laughed and said, 'I can clearly see you are not Black.' She looked at me for a long minute and then acknowledged the silliness of not having a box to be an 'other,' and those words stuck with me."

In the end Layla avoided the ticket. Exasperated, the officer tore it up and let her off with a warning. Little did that officer realize that she created a new chapter of awareness in Layla's mind about her own racial identity that existed between those two boxes.

Layla's interest in human relations, civil rights, and religious freedom intersected in college and she remained involved in student campaigns that focused on divestment and racial justice for cafeteria and janitorial workers in her college. With a newly minted degree in political science, she moved to Washington full of idealism driven in large part by the tenets of her Muslim faith. Layla believed deeply in the Islamic teaching that the racial and ethnic differences between people were not meant to divide so we could "despise one another" but rather existed so we could get to "know one another" and see the shared humanity and dignity in each other.

Layla worked on religious freedom and liberty issues at the local and national level and frequently sought to include Muslims in this work well before 9/11.

She advocated for South Asian diaspora communities to come together in solidarity around immigration reform and civic engagement campaigns, urging communities to work together in the United States despite divisions, and to collectively leverage influence in the political arena. She did this before 9/11, and there were times that engaging leaders was not only challenging; it was discouraged by most established ethnic groups involved in advocacy work in Washington. Muslims, South Asians, Arabs, and Sikhs weren't on the radar of most civil rights leadership. Making the case to organize them was at times a tough sell among established advocates.

It has not been so long since the Tsarnaev brothers set off a bomb at the end of the Boston marathon in April 2013. I remember a few things from that week that you may or may not have experienced along with me:

- Deep grief at the attack of such a family-friendly and massively attended event.
- Anxiety that the bombers would be people of color. (A fair number of people of color experience this anxiety every time there's a bombing or mass shooting. White mass murderers are seen as individuals; people of color are discussed as representatives of their race.)
- A "here we go again" feeling when I learned that Boston doctor Heba Abolaban from Syria was attacked by a man who said, "F*** you Muslims," and, "You were involved in the Boston bombings!" a day before police announced they had found a suspect.[5] (The first person they brought in, a Saudi Arabian man with burn marks on his hands, was cleared the same day as the bombing.) Dr. Abolaban was wearing a hijab, a headscarf worn by some Muslim women.
- Relief (I know; I'm not proud of that) when the suspects were literally Caucasian—from the land of the Caucusus Mountains.
- Mild horror as their religious identity became known and (you can say this was all in my head) I watched people almost visibly thinking, "Whew! They're not *really* White if they're Muslim!" and bearing witness to the marked shift in media coverage that I knew would not result in retaliations against White Muslims in the same way it would against people who "look" Muslim, bearing in mind that what the Tsarnaevs promoted bears no resemblance to the beliefs of the vast majority of Muslims in this country, be they Black, White, or Brown. Remember: Muslim is to terrorist as Christian is to KKK.

---

[5]Maria Sacchetti, "Malden woman attacked by man accusing Muslims of Marathon bombings," *Boston Globe,* April 18, 2013. Available at: http://www.boston.com/2013/04/18/malden-woman-attacked-man-accusing-muslims-marathon-bombings/goI1fmyQzBwjbt728pqqdK/story.html#sthash.QBTUphMv.dpuf.

This is what is so complicated about race and religion in America. We've talked in this book a bit about White privilege. In some ways, we also live in a country where the Christian narrative and Christianity as a religion benefits from some privilege. Privilege is always hard to see when we're the ones benefiting from it, and I, for one, am very proud of living in a country where the freedom of religion is a foundation of our constitution. So here are a couple of illustrations of the ways I benefit from being a Christian in the United States without even always being aware of it: a Christian bumper sticker on my car doesn't open me up for targeted vandalism. People who represent me in public office have a working understanding of my faith. I am never expected to speak on behalf of my whole religion. (Sometimes I do, but I usually can't fool people that all Christians believe what I do—we're too well known.) My house of worship is not likely to get burned down because people hate or distrust or fear my religion. (In the late 1990s there was a resurgence of church bombings, but they were race-based.)

Suspicion about Muslim Americans escalated to its highest levels not immediately after the terror attacks but rather several years later. The explanation is often attributed to the rise of so-called anti-terror experts who were ubiquitous in seeding doubt along with a series of questionable research reports about the incompatibility of Islam and democracy.

The goal was clear: plant seeds of distrust and fear that Muslims are inherently "the other," different not simply by cultural practice but by nature. This explanation was used repeatedly to quiet the moral challenges that the country was acting counter to its values and constitutional promises by allowing sanctioned use of torture, rendition of immigrants, and conditions at Guantanamo Bay.

Under the banner of national and homeland security, there was a call for widespread surveillance of American Muslim communities and enclaves. The power of this narrative in the public psyche became clear during Congressional hearings convened during the ten-year anniversary of 9/11 by then Homeland Security House Committee Chairman Peter King, a staunch and easily angered Republican from Long Island,

New York. The hearings convened were eerily reminiscent of the McCarthy-era campaign. Surveillance of Muslims was not a new idea and had surfaced many times before, often by right-wing groups such as the Christian Coalition. Yet it was not until 2011 that public acceptance created the needed political traction for Peter King's efforts.

A previously unlikely coalition of liberal, moderate, and progressive ethnic and religious leadership was the silver lining of this moment in history. The organization Muslim Advocates led the coalition with support from mainstream civil liberties groups and advocates who focused on everything from promoting immigration reform to Sikh civil rights. Their leadership would not have been supported or welcomed prior to 9/11, but in the face of a threat to our shared understanding of American integrity, we found common cause. The hearings led to a clarion call to people of faith and goodwill to mobilize. Representative Keith Ellison, a Muslim American and African American member of Congress from Minnesota, helped shift the discourse.

The interesting thing is that the church has some experience, albeit long ago, of being on the other side of this privilege/oppression equation. In fact, the most controversial book of the Bible, the book of Revelation, was actually written as both a warning and source of hope to Christians being persecuted by the Roman Empire because, like the Jewish community, Christians would not praise Caesar as a god, which made them dangerous in the sight of the Roman Empire, no matter how small a group they were.

Admittedly, this is not how most of us have been trained to read the book of Revelation, which is a little bit on purpose. Many centuries ago, when the canon (the formal list of books of the Bible we use today) was being established, the church was trying to get on the good side of Rome. Any idiot could read the book of Revelation and realize that the Whore of Babylon was actually Rome, and the picture John of Patmos painted of her was *not* flattering. Priests and bishops talked of cutting Revelation so they wouldn't antagonize the empire that was finally not killing them or forcing them to denounce their faith and was even considering adopting it. An early church father, Origen, decided the book was too important a part of our story to lose, so he insisted it was actually about the end times and should be kept in the canon. We also have him to thank for my favorite book, the book of James. The church wanted to ditch that one because it was too Jewish, and they did *not* want to be associated with Judaism. He said you couldn't cut a book written by *the brother of Jesus*, even though people mostly knew it wasn't actually written by the brother of Jesus.

The book of Revelation cautions churches not to deny God and Jesus even though there are huge risks to their safety and lives in staying faithful. It also acknowledges how hard it is to be on the margins, living in fear, sometimes having to worship in secret. The Roman Empire is terrifying (and seemingly invincible) as John of Patmos describes it in Revelation 13:

> And I saw a beast rising out of the sea, having ten horns and seven heads; and on its horns were ten diadems, and on its heads were blasphemous names... One of its heads seemed to have received a death-blow, but its mortal wound had been healed. In amazement the whole earth followed the beast... [A]nd they worshiped the beast, saying, "Who is like the beast, and who can fight against it?"... It opened its mouth to utter blasphemies against God, blaspheming his name and his dwelling, that is, those who dwell in heaven... [A]nd all the inhabitants of the earth will worship it, everyone whose name has not been written from the foundation of the world in the book of life of the Lamb that was slaughtered. (vv. 1, 3, 4b, 6, 8, NRSV)

Those would have been scary times to be a Christian.

So it both puzzles and saddens me that as a country we have turned Christianity into a form of privilege, of access to resources and stability, of what is "normal" or "normative." And this has intersected in disturbing ways with how we define race.

My favorite comic strip is Aaron McGruder's *Boondocks*. When it became okay again to be funny in the months following 9/11, McGruder did a comic about the fact that South Asians and Arab Americans had become the most feared ethnic groups in America. In the comic, one of the Black children asked another how he felt about this new statistic and its displacement of African Americans as the most feared group in America. The child paused for a second and then started chanting, "We're number THREE! We're number THREE!"

This is a reminder of that hierarchy of privilege. In the decade since that comic ran, anti-Muslim hate crimes have continued to remain above their pre-9/11 rates (with a particular spike of 50 percent in 2010, simultaneous to several state legislatures proposing anti-Muslim legislation). The intersection of religious discrimination, stereotyping, and racism in America today begs something of us as Christians, whose ancient heritage is born of being stereotyped and discriminated against.

There are moments of hope and possibility for us. We adapt and we learn. The civil rights groups with leaders who once questioned Layla's efforts to organize and engage Muslim, South Asian, Arab, and Sikh community groups are now championing efforts to battle racial and religious profiling. Muslim groups such as Muslim Advocates have created and led multi-faith and multi-ethnic policy and advocacy coalitions to challenge anti-Muslim bias that was fueling a series of fear-based congressional inquiries. The leadership of the nation's preeminent civil rights groups now includes senior posts held by Muslims and South Asians at an unprecedented level.

The nation's most influential progressive think tank, the Center for American Progress, released a groundbreaking report, "Fear, Inc.," to galvanize awareness in the big tent about the dangers of the anti-Muslim movement and then need to challenge it. The lessons and message of "Fear, Inc." generated national attention and is helping change the conversation and exposes the bigotry behind the state-sanctioned religious profiling that guts the First Amendment.

Closer to home, Layla participated in my ordination. She wrote and delivered an ordination vow alongside a rabbi calling me to a lifetime commitment to protect the rights and wellbeing of all people of faith and goodwill. It was an easy vow for me to make, with the memory still fresh of my father's safety being under threat in the days following 9/11. But it was an equally easy vow to make as someone who has studied the book of Revelation and knows that a people who have lived in fear for their beliefs cannot in good conscience participate in a culture that allows people to live in fear for their beliefs.

Insha'Allah (if it be God's will), America may one day be the Beloved Community where all are free to worship without fear.

CHAPTER QUESTIONS

1. Read the story of the good Samaritan and substitute "the good Muslim." What does that evoke for you?
2. Are there any mosques or Islamic cultural centers you could visit? Has your congregation reached out to the Muslim community?
3. Are there any common goals that your congregation and the Muslim community could work on? Could the Muslim community be invited to any event your congregation sponsors?
4. How did this chapter make you rethink your own memory of 9/11?
5. How did this chapter make you rethink your reading of the book of Revelation?
6. What does supporting people of a different religion when they are persecuted have to do with the Beloved Community?

8

We Are Each Others' ~~Victims~~ *Siblings*

"I don't believe in charity. I believe in solidarity. Charity is vertical, so it's humiliating. It goes from the top to the bottom. Solidarity is horizontal. It respects the other and learns from the other. I have a lot to learn from other people."

—Eduardo Galeano

"We cannot afford to be separate. We have to see that all of us are in the same boat."

—Dorothy Height

Tai Amri used to work at a school that was predominantly Latin@, but there were some Black kids and some Asian American kids. Two in particular stand out to him: fourth-grade Vietnamese twins. The other kids picked on both of them, "You're Chinese! Ching Chong!" which still makes Tai Amri a little crazy: "They *weren't* Chinese!" What was different, though, was that one was an athletic, gregarious boy who liked to play soccer. So other than the teasing that all kids got in some form or variation (anyone who "nostalgizes" little kids does not remember how mean they can be), he was well liked and accepted. The other twin was a pudgy, shy girl. All she ever got was the teasing. When I sat down to talk with Tai Amri, a thirty-something African American man, and his colleague Laura (pronounced LOW-rah in Spanish), a thirty-something Jewish-Chilean woman, I asked them if we could talk about the way minorities got pitted against each other. He responded, "I can't separate race and gender and fat phobia" and shared the story of those two Vietnamese twins.

Part of that story is just that kids can be mean, and we make a mistake in acting as if children are completely pure. Part of the story is that our identities are multiple, and different aspects of who we are can keep certain doors open when other aspects would otherwise have closed those doors. (See chapter twelve on intersectionality.) But part of that story is about how hard it is to be a small minority, even in an all-minority school, and any advantage you have matters if you're that minority. (The final part of that story is that Tai Amri suffers from an uncontrollable case of empathy. He can't help being an empath and a mystic. When we pastored a church together, I told prospective student ministers that he and I covered the full range of liberation theology: I covered the Huey Newton end of the spectrum and he covered the Howard Thurman end of the spectrum.)

A minor obsession of mine, and part of what brought me into the work of racial reconciliation, is the way that oppressed communities are pitted against each other and fight for scraps. I see it in the way that, during the L.A. riots, poor Black people in Watts destroyed Korean businesses in retaliation for racist White police officers beating Rodney King almost to death. I also see it in the way my own South Asian and larger Asian community's business owners, not always able to get loans for businesses in affluent communities, sometimes unconsciously but often willingly exploit poor Black people with corner stores with high markups and promotion of addictive substances that they know will harm the community. And I have heard them justify it by perpetuating stereotypes that feed their contempt of their clientele and encourage customers in turn to hate and blame "Indians and Ay-rabs" for their plight, as a man

I worked with in west Chicago referred to the 7-11 owners in his neighborhood.

John D. Marquez in his book, *Black-Brown Solidarity,* notes how tensions specifically between the Black and Latin@ communities are framed publicly in contrast to what is actually happening:[1]

> The literature of black-Latino/a conflict often manufactures, exaggerates, or overlooks data regarding the impact of the Latino/a boom on black unemployment, Latino/a voting habits, and black and Latino/a gang violence. In 2008 it was widely suggested that Latinos/as would not support the presidential campaign of Barack Obama because he was black. Ultimately, strong Latino/a support has been cited as one reason Obama won that campaign over Republican candidate John McCain. There are also widespread misconceptions regarding black versus Latino/a competition over jobs. Although Latinos/as and especially those who are immigrants are commonly depicted as stealing jobs from blacks, the steady loss of black jobs in recent decades has been the result of industrial downsizing and the outsourcing of manufacturing jobs to the global South. Moreover, the most influential factor in high rates of black unemployment has been shown to be deeply rooted anti-black stereotypes harbored by some employers. By comparison, increased competition for jobs created by Latino/a population growth has had only a minimal effect on black joblessness.

In addition to the data, I think about the heartbreaking stories I read about African Americans being displaced in the wake of Hurricane Katrina while Latin@ migrant workers lived in awful conditions, in tents on hillsides, as they were sub-sub-subcontracted at poor wages to rebuild. Both

---

[1]John D. Marquez, Black-Brown *Solidarity: Racial Politics in the New Gulf South* (Austin, University of Texas Press, 2013), 26.

communities were being mistreated, and there was no venue for them to figure out together the larger issues of economic injustice and racism that created both the displacement and the horrifically low wages and poor living conditions.

I think about the Black pastors coalition in Los Angeles that invited the Minutemen, a predominantly White, armed vigilante group that hunt people crossing the border from Mexico to the United States, as guest speakers following the first massive Latin@ immigrant rights march in L.A. in 2006. The timing of the invitation had everything to do with Latin@s and Blacks both feeling that their future was completely under threat and suspecting the other of contributing to that threat.

I also think of the amazing work to build relationships between the Latin@ and Black clergy in Los Angeles, and between Black and Korean clergy following the riots after the unjust Rodney King verdict in 1992. Those coalitions continue to this day both in my Oakland community and in Los Angeles. However, I know that work is hard work, and it requires constantly regrouping and remembering that God unites them even while they feel unsafe with one another at times.

And so those tensions show up on the playground, in the classroom, and in the after-school program at an all-minority school. The way Tai Amri's supervisor, Laura, sees it, the kids learn it from their parents: "I hear parents—laborers, brown people, hard working people, saying out of pocket stuff about Black people without thinking about it." Regarding her program's role at the school, "It's kinetic energy—it keeps going until the momentum is broken. A virus needs a host," and part of the purpose of the after-school program at her school as she sees it is to stop the kinetic energy of racial hostility.

It's part of why she hired Tai Amri, one of four African American people working in the building (along with one teacher, one janitor, and another after-school program leader). "I prayed on it a lot, and my heart told me to. I was completely transparent with him: We're building a community here. We're the heart. We're building a paradigm together."

Latin@s, both immigrants and those who have lived and worked in the community for generations, compose the neighborhood where Tai Amri and Laura work. Many work multiple jobs. Poverty is high. Housing costs are high. Crime is not infrequent. In fact, the school is very near the major street in Oakland where sex trafficking is most visibly present, with young girls and women walking the streets all day and night. When Tai Amri did a session with his class on preventing bullying one day, he taught them the word "ally." He asked them who in the neighborhood needed an ally. One of the first groups they named was "the girls who have to stand on the corner."

At Tai Amri's current school, Spanish is the dominant language, which actually makes things simpler. At his previous school, "you had to *try* to leave people out… I saw more racism amongst the kids because you had to specifically say, 'This game is for kids who speak Spanish' [which intentionally excluded English-speaking students, particularly Black students], whereas here you don't have to make those stipulations [because almost every student is from the same racial background]. I do have more fear that I'm the only black person these kids know." Tai Amri knows that, even if he challenges their stereotypes, he may become in their minds the exception that proves the rule.

It's obvious that the kids in this school (and in Tai Amri's previous school) have the capacity for empathy. It's obvious that they didn't make up all of the racial tensions themselves. And Tai Amri can point out lots of instances in which racial tensions have shown up between kids (more so at his previous school, but here also). And, as Laura mentioned, it's obvious that they're picking it up from their parents.

So where are the parents picking up their hostilities about one another? Tai Amri remembers that, growing up, "My parents didn't condone racism. But I watched a lot of comedians who traded in racial stereotypes. And I'm thinking about *Do the Right Thing* (Spike Lee's groundbreaking film on Black-White racial tensions from the 1990s). It's one of my favorite films, but it's also where I learned it was okay to make fun of Asians." So media portrayal is one of those places.

"And we're in each other's face all the time," adds Laura, who has grown up in east Oakland. "We're crowded in, so we're gonna fight with our neighbor." The concentration of poverty and the population density add to tensions.

"Also, we're made to compete with each other," says Tai Amri: "'Look how easy it was for you to get a loan.' So the anger's at the community we think is discriminated against less, and not at the people who created the program that perpetuates discrimination."

In my own work advocating for affordable housing, I have definitely heard Black and White affordable housing residents complain that Asian residents dominate a particular building culturally and linguistically, and I have heard Latin@ clergy complain that there are no resources for their incredibly poor community because Black people have more access to social services. I wouldn't say any of those suppositions is actually true (although undocumented workers on whom our economy relies do not have any access to affordable housing, and many of those workers are Latin@). However, this distrust has no way of being resolved, and it simmers. It does not get addressed and refocused toward an economy that does not provide for the least, the last, and the lost, or for the hard working people who serve as the backbone of our economy but struggle to keep a roofs over their heads. I want to be clear, I'm not saying there aren't legitimate tensions between people of color; I'm just saying that I think a lot of those tensions could be addressed in the right forum so that people of color would be better aware of one another's lived experiences.

Not all people of color see this the same way I do. I recently co-facilitated an anti-racism training for Asian, Asian American, and Pacific Islander Christians. I co-facilitated it with an amazing African American trainer so we could model solidarity between API and African American communities. We shared the history of Asians in America and showed how civil rights work of Asians throughout history had made life better for Latin@s and Blacks, and how their civil rights campaigns had actually made our lives in this country better throughout history. We created space that allowed a first-generation immigrant to share how her sense of safety in her neighborhood had been destroyed months before by some guys on bikes who were bored and decided to make xenophobic remarks and threaten to beat her up. Some of the first-generation immigrants said they had not realized they had any common cause with Latin@s and Blacks because their whole experience of America had been how to get along with and stay under the radar of White people. Pacific Islanders talked about their experiences of harassment by police.

But most of the middle class East Asian second-generation Americans weren't buying it. No stories about internment camps or Vincent Chin[2] or illegal deportations of South Asians after 9/11 convinced them that the issue of racism had anything to do with them. This broke my heart because I saw a lack of empathy in their willingness to ignore the stories they had heard from first-generation immigrants and Pacific Islanders. It broke my heart because they were locating themselves in relationship with the privilege of Whiteness and also making the leap to say that their proximity to White acceptance meant they had no responsibility toward Blacks, Latin@s, and Native Americans who did experience quantifiable and qualified racism. It made me ache for their future selves who will confront the "bamboo ceiling" that limits leadership opportunities for Asian Americans due to subtle but prevalent stereotypes about the gifts and weaknesses of the "model minority" that they are likely too young to have become aware of at this point in their careers.[3] But it did not shock me, because part of what is so complicated about racism is that it affects different groups (and even different subgroups) differently, while our options for analyzing oppression tend to be binary. That binary didn't resonate with the relatively privileged young adults at the training, particularly with the strong pressure to aspire to

---

[2]See www.nytimes.com/2012/06/23/opinion/why-vincent-chin-matters.html.

[3]For more information about the "bamboo ceiling," read the transcript of the interview on National Public Radio: "Does the 'Bamboo Ceiling' Shut Asian Americans out of top jobs?" May 23, 2014. http://www.npr.org/2014/05/23/315129852/does-a-bamboo-ceiling-shut-asian-americans-out-of-top-jobs

acceptance within White society rather than developing solidarity with other, even more marginalized or oppressed groups.[4]

I defined racism in a previous chapter as race prejudice plus the misuse of power by systems and institutions. I also believe that while most of the White people I know do not want to benefit from White privilege, our systems and institutions are set up to preserve power and privilege for White people, whether they want it or not. I do not believe that any group of people of color has the same kind of privilege in America. I do believe that part of what keeps systemic racism in place is a complicated racial hierarchy that immigrants in particular are not aware of because they are entering a narrative that is, quite literally, foreign to us and which we work hard to fit ourselves into. As a result, we often perpetuate systemic racism while simultaneously being limited by it. In a context in which the history of Black / White relations dominates the limited race conversations available to us, a lot of immigrants don't think the conversation about race has much to do with us, and we rarely have opportunities to hear any other narrative about race relations that seems to have anything to do with us. Similarly, immigration conversations on the national front rarely bring multiple racial groups to the table. As a result, we each take to our corners, often not interacting with each other, forming opinions based on caricatures in the media or bad experiences of one another. We have bad experiences of some White folks, too, but the media gives us a wide array of representations of White people, and only (to borrow again from Chimamanda Adichie) a single story of one another. There are few places for us to wrestle with our own and one another's complexities.

---

[4]My colleague Timothy Murphy, Executive Director of Progressive Christians Uniting, recently introduced me to the work of political philosopher Iris Marion Young, who suggests that we should acknowledge different types of oppression as substantively different, rather than conflating them for the sake of building solidarity, since the solidarity that builds is fairly shallow. The categories she suggests in her book *Justice and the Politics of Difference* are: exploitation, marginalization, powerlessness, cultural imperialism, and violence. Young doesn't argue for a hierarchy but an acknowledgment that not all forms of oppression are the same.

Tai Amri sometimes feels the pressure of being the only Black man that many of the students work with: "Since Black people are not the majority in this community, I wonder what are their experiences of Black people? I'm sure they have a lot of negative experiences and I might be the first positive experience. I may be the exception that proves the rule or I might just get lumped in with their negative associations before I get to prove myself as an individual." Then he remembers what is different in the school he's at now compared to last year: "I think of the time I had a supervisor who was less aware of those race dynamics. She didn't recognize what it was like to be Black or even Asian in that school. She didn't recognize how much targeting some of those racial minorities faced. So I told Laura I can't work in a place where that's not acknowledged. And she acknowledges it all the time. There was only one Black kid in the program for a long time and he had a hard time; now there's three more. But also, I think the difference in the structure we have means he can call people out—even me… That would never have happened at my last school."

"And that's because you're here," says Laura. "Instead of feeling the pressure, you are making a difference."

Tai Amri and Laura both have a hard road, creating a safe space for poor children of immigrants where they feel 100 percent valued while preparing those same children for a world where they will not always be valued. Laura notes that, as poor as the school is, there's a bit of a bubble for the kids where everyone's experience is like theirs and they all speak the same language; when they get to middle school, they will be far worse resourced and statistically far more prone to being pushed out of the education track and into the criminal track. The city of Oakland, like many cities, has had to establish a panel specifically addressing the school-to-prison pipeline of Black and Brown Boys both dropping out and being pushed out of public schools. Statistics show this starts in elementary school, long before the boys could have proven they cannot be educated. The challenge, Laura says, is to "intersperse some gentle moments of truth while trying not to disrupt their innocence. It's a very gentle craft."

It's a craft not every educator masters. At Tai Amri's previous school, he worked with a child who still haunts me. One day Tai Amri was encouraging them to talk about their dreams for the future. "I dream that one day butterflies will come back to Oakland," he said by means of illustration.

"That's stupid," the child responded, "butterflies HATE Oakland."

Tai Amri's heart broke for the child who was carrying so much hurt so young. He had been disciplined more times than anyone could count, and before the end of the year, the director of the after-school program reached the end of her patience and suspended him. "What second grader has done something so bad he should get suspended?" Tai Amri asked rhetorically. This is what the laying of the first pipe in the school-to-prison pipeline for Black boys and men looks like.[5] I find myself reflecting on the Scripture of the man at the side of the pool at Bethsaida, and I'll tell you why. As Tai Amri, Laura, and I shared a cup of coffee together, we started talking about how to foster healthier communications between people of different races and cultures, and what they are doing in their school on that issue. Laura said, "People need to come to listen, but humbly remembering someone else doesn't owe it to you to teach you. So I ask myself, in the work I'm doing, 'Are we moving forward in a way that helps others heal?' What's intense about this work, though, is that right now we're still in the healing stage and we don't even know it."

You'd think the man at Bethsaida knew he needed healing. He was sitting by a pool said to have healing properties for the lucky person who hopped in first when the water "stirred."

I love the dramatic language when Jesus shows up and talks to the man and says to him, "Will ye be healed?" or "Do you want to be healed?" I like to imagine a little bit of parity between them: Jesus clearly isn't a well-heeled rabbi of the

---

[5]The radio show *This American Life* recently did a story about the disproportionate punishment of Black children throughout their educational careers on the episode entitled "Is This Working?" on October 17, 2014. http://www.thisamericanlife.org/radio-archives/episode/538/is-this-working.

temple or a wealthy elite, so the man, I like to imagine, can talk to him a little more "brother-to-brother." "It's hard out here, man," I imagine him saying. "I can't catch a break. I keep trying to get into the pool, but people with friends or connections or better functioning limbs always beat me in there." He leads with his wounds, with the many ways he has been stopped from getting to those healing waters. That's what we do when we're still in the healing stage and don't even know it. We lead with our wounds.

I have previously used this passage to talk about congregational transformation. I've talked about how Jesus doesn't care much about our excuses. He just wants to know if we seriously, really want to be healed. But in listening to Laura, I find myself thinking about the ways communities of color stay wounded, maybe not even realizing we're still in the healing stage and don't even know it.

And Jesus knows what that's like. He's from a community on the margins, not treated well at all by the empire that's oppressing them, and a community also that picks at itself from the inside, so that the poorest of the poor suffer even more. We often blame communities of color for that. A recent Internet meme said, "We talk about people of color acting like crabs in a barrel, pulling each other down so the other crabs won't escape, without discussion of the fact that a barrel is not the natural environment for a crab." What happens between people of color does not happen in a vacuum. It happens in the thick smog of White supremacy that we all breathe every day, usually without realizing that it is in our lungs, all of us.

So Jesus lets the man dispense with the institutional solution, the system-sanctioned pool that only heals one person a day, and usually a person with at least *some* resources available. Jesus creates another way out: "Pick up your mat and walk."

Now, that's what makes it a miracle story. Picking up our mat and walking will look a lot different today. Our wounds have sometimes been formed over generations, and while we need help from one another for all of us to stand, we've also been trained to see one another as the reasons we're by the side of the pool and not in it. And we may actually have done some of the harming of one another. We're still in in the healing stage and don't even know it. Therein, though, lies the Beloved Community today.

Here's what I think it might look like for people of color to participate in picking up one another's mats and helping one another walk, even as we ourselves are in the healing stage: it looks like Tai Amri helping the kids he works with pick up their mats, kids who will likely be the majority in this nation by 2042: "I'm just hoping that what I'm doing is planting seeds for the world where they're actually the majority and where they can speak truth to power and feel 'I have agency and deserve power and know the avenues to affect change.' The whole majority/minority conversation—I don't know how to have that conversation with them, but the sense that 'you can change the world,' that I can do."

It looks like all of us recognizing how *other groups* can't get into the healing waters at Bethsaida and helping them pick up their mats instead. Tai Amri and Laura both talk about understanding one another's histories and making connections: "It is not any leap for me," says Tai Amri, "to see the similarities between the border and the underground railroad, 'maquiladoras' and sharecropping. I didn't grow up knowing about that, but as soon as I heard about it I thought, 'Whoa, that is the same thing.'" And that's part of why Tai Amri and Laura can have each other's backs and foster up a new way of understanding within the children they work with. When I talk with Laura and Tai Amri, I picture a world where the Dreamers and the Dream Defenders and 18 Million Rising help each other get to the healing waters in Bethsaida.

And, most hopefully, it looks like children shaped early into helping one another to pick up their mats or to carry each other. Tai Amri often jokes that, if he worked with youth and young adults (my passion), he would feel much more fatalistic about the future. With children, it is possible to create a path of deeper compassion in them that may stay with them despite what they hear on TV or from their parents (although he fears for them when they get to the bullying capital that is middle school). "That's why I work with four-year-olds," he explains. "No matter how prejudiced their parents, they don't see a scary black man. They see someone who's smiling and wants to play with them."

I've seen three butterflies in Oakland this summer. Every time I've seen one, I've prayed for that little boy, that Tai Amri's love will stay with him as he faces a world steering him toward a life of pain and little opportunity. I pray that the Beloved Community will be his, and I pray that he'll also get to see those butterflies and delight in them.

CHAPTER QUESTIONS

1. How have you previously seen divisions between communities of color discussed? Did anything come up in this chapter that made you think differently?
2. What do you think about the different categories of oppression listed in the footnotes of this chapter? How could those categories help people hear each other's experiences of oppression differently?
3. What do you think of the argument that conflicts between communities of color are also influenced by the country's narrative of creating more opportunities for White communities?
4. What did this interpretation of the story of the Man at Bethsaida make you think about differently?
5. What does the issue of the school-to-prison pipeline have to do with the Beloved Community?

9

Navigating Privilege

"After all, acknowledging unfairness then calls decent people forth to correct those injustices. And since most persons are, at their core, decent folks, the need to ignore evidence of injustice is powerful: To do otherwise would force whites to either push for change (which they would perceive as against their interests) or live consciously as hypocrites who speak of freedom and opportunity but perpetuate a system of inequality. The irony of American history is the tendency of good white Americans to presume racial innocence. Ignorance of how we are shaped racially is the first sign of privilege. In other words, it is a privilege to ignore the consequences of race in America."

—Tim Wise

"Just then a lawyer stood up to test Jesus. 'Teacher,' he said, 'what must I do to inherit eternal life?' He said to him, 'What is written in the law? What do you read there?' He answered, 'You shall love the Lord your God with all your heart, and with all your soul, and with all your strength, and with all your mind; and your neighbor as yourself.' And he said to him, 'You have given the right answer; do this, and you will live.'

But wanting to justify himself, he asked Jesus, 'And who is my neighbor?'" —Luke 10:25–29

(NRSV)

When I was twenty-six, I got to interview Jonathan Kozol. For people who care about social inequity, this was like seeing the Beatles at their Candlestick Park concert. He's written such books as *Rachel and Her Children,* about homeless families; *Savage Inequalities,* about the limited opportunities our children get in urban public schools; and the book I was interviewing him about: *Ordinary Resurrections,* stories of hope from Mott Haven, the poorest neighborhood in the United States.

I was getting ready to go to seminary, and I was feeling called to urban ministry. My incredibly supportive boyfriend who was thrilled I was responding to God's call, had come up poor and urban, his Gap ad appearance notwithstanding. "But I think you really want to look at suburban ministry," he suggested, adding, not unkindly, "What exactly do you think you have the right to say to poor urban people of color?"

So I asked Jonathan Kozol, a Jewish intellectual, about his work to integrate the Boston public schools during the civil rights movement. I even told him why I was asking, and he shared the following story (as I recall it): "When I first got involved in civil rights work, I would show up to meetings of poor Black people, and I'd use simple words and slang and try not to stand out too much. Finally one of the community leaders pulls me aside and says, 'Jonathan, you don't help this movement by hiding who you are; I mean, you went to *Harvard*. Use *that* to help. Be *yourself* when you're standing with us.' Some people get so paralyzed by their privilege they don't help anyone. Just be who you are and honor who other people are and get the work done."

I was thinking about that interview as I sat down to talk with my friend Brooke. Brooke grew up with a great view of what another of my central-Illinois-raised friends describes as the "sea of succotash," endless fields of corn and soybeans. Raised by a single mom who worked as a teacher's aide for children with developmental disabilities, Brooke lived in a mostly White neighborhood in Champaign, Illinois. If you want a glimpse into why I think she's such an amazing human being, take in this little detail: Brooke played on an all boys' hockey team from the ages of four to thirteen.

That team might have had something to do with the work she engages in today: the team was called the Chiefs (in tribute to the University of Illinois football team, the Illini, named after the Indigenous people on whose land the university stands). Brooke remembers her mother raising concerns that the name of the kids' team was a racially insensitive term. Her family identifies as White. Her mother doesn't have a history of civil rights work. So I'm curious about why, when no one else gave a second thought to the Chiefs' name and logo (a silhouette of a forward-leaning ice skater with a headdress), Brooke's mother felt the need to speak out. "I asked her that later in life," says Brooke, "and she said, 'If people [in this case Native Americans] tell you something hurts them, you believe them. If you're the one doing the hurting, you don't get to decide whether they *should* feel hurt.'"[1]

Brooke would end up getting much more involved in this exact issue when she joined the protests at the University of Illinois about the football and basketball team mascot "Chief Illiniwek." "I can't remember experiences before that campaign of having been exposed to real interaction with Native American culture or people. What I heard from Native peoples in the course of solidarity organizing was that the sheer presence of the 'Chief' made it such a hostile environment to be Native American that some Native people in the community chose to pass for White. A lot of people while I was growing up may not have brought that part of their identity up when interacting with me."

Brooke went on to explain that, as a land grant institution, the University of Illinois stood on land that was originally native land, taken by the federal government, and eventually turned into a public institution. "There is an assumption by local White people that there are no more Native Americans

[1]The issue of using Native American names for sports teams continues to be debated, but many people (myself included) believe that this is an illustration of "impact matters more than intent." When Native American communities express hurt that their current-day culture has been erased by, at best, caricatures of a fictionalized people and, at worst, racist and pejorative representations of their culture, it is best for us, who have benefitted from generations of mistreatment of this nation's first people, to honor their request.

on that land. Many White local folks would say, 'Because Native people are dead and gone, this is the only way we have to hold onto the history and legacy.' And there would be real live Native Americans in the flesh conveying that they are not dead; this is their culture and language. This is the caricature of their history that we've created. This makes it hard to raise their children with their cultural identity, it hurts their community. The best way for us to honor them is to listen. And they were asking us to stop. And that was a clash." Over years and years, Brooke saw people begin to accept this new information and understand that the "Chief" might be hurtful instead of meaningful to a people who were real and alive instead of dead and mythologized on White terms.

As an aside, Brooke is a layperson with a deep spirituality whose mother instilled values around justice and fairness and faith as being interconnected. "When I was a kid my mother said, 'God is a verb.' She never studied liberation theology, but she said, 'Maybe God's a person, but what matters more is how we treat people as if they matter.' When I repeated this in Presbyterian Sunday school, they called my mom to express their concern that what I was learning at home didn't fit with what I was learning at church. Specifically, the Bible study leader said that this belief was theologically incorrect, to which my mom replied, 'She's thinking and there's nothing wrong with thinking,' so we didn't go back." As an adult, Brooke heard a song while visiting Guatemala and immediately called her mom to say, "That thing you taught me as a child—there's a song about it!" Written by Ricardo Arjona in Spanish, it says in part,

> Jesus is more than a simple and flat theory,
> What are you doing, brother, reading the Bible all day?
> What is written there is bound in love,
> Come on, go and practice it.
> Jesus, my brothers, is a verb, not a noun.[2]

Today Brooke brings environmental groups and unions

---

[2]The song, in Spanish, is called "Jesus Verbo No Sustantivo."

together to create jobs that pay fairly and help the planet at the same time. She's one of the best organizers I know, and I wonder what motivates her to stay in the work she does and also what it means for her as a middle class White woman to be engaged in work primarily with poor brown-skinned workers. I wonder about this because, in my line of work, as I stated earlier, we talk about something called "White Privilege," a phrase that causes a visceral reaction from some people who feel unjustly accused of something, and a resigned acceptance from others who have learned to accept the moniker but feel pretty well crushed under it.

Again, here's how I would define White privilege: it's all of the invisible perks of being White that White people didn't ask for (and many don't want) but they get anyhow. In Peggy McIntosh's famous article, "Unpacking the Invisible Knapsack,"[3] she lists some examples. A few that spring to mind for me (borrowing from the "This is White Privilege" Tumblr structure) are:

White privilege is not being followed around a store out of the assumption you will steal something.

White privilege is not having to teach your children how to avoid undue attention from the police.

White privilege is never having people question whether you are really American, no matter how long ago your family immigrated to this country. (This is true for day-to-day interactions and also for laws in states such as Arizona, where you can be pulled over for not looking American, with all that implies.)

Brooke benefits from White privilege, and yet I don't generally experience her as either being defensive about that privilege or denying it, nor do I experience her as perpetually apologizing for it in the midst of her work. She is really clear on why it matters and why people avoid addressing it: "People are scared to talk about race. So we talk about it as class or organizing strategy instead. Different people don't talk about race for different reasons and in different contexts.

---

[3]Available at https://www.isr.umich.edu/home/diversity/resources/white-privilege.pdf.

Sometimes we're not sure race is the thing at play. Or we know it is and yet don't know how to isolate it among other factors. Sometimes we don't want to experience retribution. We're often afraid we're going to make a mistake or use the wrong words." She's also really clear (and this is so important and so overlooked) about what would help us do the work of addressing White privilege (and any privilege) in healthier ways: "Part of why this happens is we're not in deep and authentic relationship with each other, which is an essential foundation that allows us to be honest with each other when we've done something that perpetuates racism or other stereotypes, and to experience being the one to be called out as a call to confront our own racism to strengthen our collective fight for liberation without getting paralyzed or leaving the movement. So much of our organizing we do in such a hurry so the only connection we have is having been in meetings."

When I asked Brooke how she avoids the paralysis of White guilt while still acknowledging White privilege, she reflected on the following: "Sure, paralysis is a force and I can feel it pushing on me. But, there's a stronger pull that comes from why I got into the movement and why I stay in the movement. And it's not that I don't ever have paralyzing thoughts/feelings, but that there's a pull grounded in my own experiences that is stronger. I think there's a difference in coming to the movement from a book or a class, [and] when you went through something and you can connect it to a real movement. Whenever it gets hard, you can come back to that."

For Brooke, in a very real way, organizing saved her life. Like one in six women on her campus at the time, Brooke was sexually assaulted in college. Many women know the Post-Traumatic Stress Disorder that can accompany that experience. "I was struggling to get out of bed, see myself as a worthwhile person, not freak out," she says. She got involved with Take Back the Night organizing and then began to see how the work around equal rights and dignity for women connected with poor Black parents seeing their children grow up with high rates of asthma because the waste incinerators in town were placed within two blocks of each other directly in the Black community. She saw firsthand how that was connected with civil liberties when she watched her neighbor, a Palestinian rights activist, get led away in handcuffs after 9/11 with no one knowing how to reach him or find out what had happened to him.

So what keeps her in the movement is this learning from her own experience: "The lesson I eventually took from the experience of being assaulted was that even when someone has complete control over your body, there are two things you still control: a belief that it's not your fault and a decision to fight back. When I saw other people and communities who had had everything taken from them, but who similarly insisted on seeing the hardship in their lives as tied to systemic injustice and who had decided to fight, I wanted to be out there in the world fighting alongside them for their lives and for mine."

In the midst of moments where people reflect her unconscious privilege back to her, she acknowledges hurt feelings. And she recognizes that what's worse than hurt feelings is the world as it is instead of the world as it could be. She remembers what brought her to this work and chooses, again, to give herself to it. And she also remembers the times she's needed to call out people she loves when they act in ways hurtful to women and knows that she would hate for them to walk away from the work because of that one issue. After all, walking away is not a choice everyone can make. It's the easy choice, and it's a choice born of the same privilege Brooke is seeking to ultimately eliminate.

The weird and tragic part of this story is that it is also about the costs of Whiteness. When Brooke worked on the campaign to get rid of Chief Illiniwek as mascot for the University of Illinois, she talked with people who told her that, without the Chief, they had no identity. Generations of immigrants have come to this country, and many of the ones who *could* assimilate into White society had to check their rich cultural heritage at the door. In other Indigenous-people-turned-mascots debates today, a disturbing amalgam of entitlement and fear shows up in people's defense of, say, a certain Washington, D.C., football team, so that being told their team name is hurtful becomes "threatening," while actual threats to Native American activists' lives and safety remain ignored.[4]

About six months ago, a clergy colleague of mine from the deep South said to me, "I hate that you're in my head."

"What are you talking about?" I asked. (We don't talk all that often face-to-face.)

"The last time I saw you (at least a year before), you said something like, 'Privilege looks a lot like thinking your intentions matter more than your impact.' And now that pops into my head *all the time*," he said, half-appreciative, and maybe more than half-exhausted.

Part of the reason I'm struck by Brooke's life story is that, as Tim Wise points out, the United States is set up mostly to protect White privilege, and at the same time most people are good people. If you keep poking at the issue of White privilege you have to do something about it, and that puts you in the midst of work that not a lot of White people are doing. And it puts you in a world with people of color (who don't get a choice about whether to recognize racism) who are frustrated with how often White people don't roll up their sleeves. So the ones who do join with us might get a few more bruises than they deserve for putting themselves out there like they have—which is why Tim Wise argues that a lot of White people don't go deep often enough. It is because once you go too far, it requires a radical life change

---

[4]This arose most tangibly and publicly when *The Daily Show* featured a surprise debate between Washington, D.C., football team fans and Native American activists seeking to change the team's current name because the term "Redskin" alludes to the bounty early settlers could collect from the government if they killed and scalped a Native person. A description of the episode can be found here: http://www.washingtonpost.com/local/the-daily-show-springs-showdown-with-native-americans-on-redskins-fans/2014/09/19/c6c5f936-3f73-11e4-b03f-de718edeb92f_story.html, and insights into the actual threats the Native American activists experienced are described here: http://www.salon.com/2014/09/29/what_the_daily_shows_redskins_segment_didnt_show/.

and a commitment to change the way things are.

This tension between wanting to be good and not wanting to confront an overwhelming system that preserves White privilege has shown up a great deal in the days and months following the shooting of Michael Brown (and bringing attention to Eric Garner's death in New York and John Crawford's death in Cincinnati and Tamir Rice's death in Cleveland). I have watched many friends explain away the death of Michael Brown and others, because the alternative is to begin to look at all these deaths not as isolated incidents with just enough muddiness to allow for the benefit of the doubt but as part of the fabric of a society that protects White privilege at any cost (which is why the Black Lives Matter campaign emerged—as a reminder that Black lives actually don't matter in this society). Police officers live in the same culture as the rest of us—a culture that trains us to start with the assumption of Black men being threatening. The reason grand juries almost never indict officers is that they imagine if they were the officer, they would be just as afraid of the Black man the officer shot. The reason grand juries almost always indict other defendants is that they imagine that they would never have committed the crime the defendant is accused of. Our system is broken, and our system is propped up by people who understand themselves to be good and who maybe aren't ready to confront the whole system.

And I find myself thinking about the parable of the good Samaritan. "So who is my neighbor?" the lawyer challenges Jesus. And Jesus tells the story you know so well, of the man walking a dangerous road who gets mugged and left for dead. A priest and a scribe both walk by without helping—people of his own race at a time of real racial tensions, and people of his faith at a time Jewish people had to stick together as some of the only monotheists in a world led by a Caesar who expected to be worshiped as a great god among many. And then the Jewish man is rescued and cared for by a Samaritan; a man from Samaria who doesn't believe that God lives in the temple but that God lives on Mt. Gerizim. This is a man from a faith deeply disdained by Jewish people. At the end of the story, once the lawyer has been forced to publicly concede that a Samaritan, at least in this story, is a good guy, Jesus says, "Go and do likewise."

We usually assume Jesus means "go be like the good Samaritan." But I think about Brooke. I think about her sitting on the front porch of poorly paid immigrant truck drivers and sharing a beer late at night and learning about their children, partly because she's a good organizer and partly because she loves and is made better by those workers. I think of her standing alongside Charlene Teeters, the Indigenous woman who would bring her daughter to University of Illinois games to remind the fans that there were real live Indians still living in the community who were hurt by the mascot "Chief Illiniwek" and how he erased the real lives and culture of the people. I picture Brooke listening to workers talking about how they care about the air their children breathe as much as their wages and health care. And I think she might have gotten Jesus' message better than the rest of us.

Perhaps Jesus was saying: "Recognize the humanity, the deep capacity for kindness, the potential greatness of this people you have been taught to believe are inferior. Accept their gifts. Do not malign them, and do not let others perpetuate the lie that they are inferior." Perhaps Jesus' message, delivered to a person with relative privilege within the Jewish community, was for people with privilege to locate themselves in the man at the side of the road. (And to recognize that when you're down and out, "your own people" aren't always the ones who have your back.)

I've written a lot about the "divide and conquer" strategy that preserves a lot of power for a few people by keeping the rest of us caught up in small things that distract us from both our similarities and the shared ways in which our rights have been taken from us. Brooke has had some of the same experiences. She mentioned, somewhat confessionally, that it might be problematic that White folks gravitate to and stay involved with campaigns for people of color when "one of the most useful things we can do is organize our own folks; for me, White middle class folks. In every society, those in power exploit certain classes and races, and choose to buy the silence and consent of other classes / races. In the U.S. today, the 1 percent, which is unsurprisingly almost entirely White, has bought the silence of poor and middle class White folks with racism. And that racism prevents us from seeing that we as White folks of the 99 percent have more in common with people of color from the 99 percent than we do with the White 1 percent. Racism keeps us from rebelling against the forces that deny us decent housing, education, and health care. As White organizers, we should see part of our role as fighting that racism in the White community and helping our White brothers and sisters see their common cause with struggling families of all colors. But, we, myself included, aren't doing enough of that work because it is hard, hard work."

When Brooke was still in central Illinois, she organized in a very poor county for basic health access. "I was working with poor White people with one toothbrush in a family of six, one of the last counties to get a health department for immunizations. And I was working with a growing immigrant population that didn't have Spanish language services at the health center. White folks' racism would get in the way of them being able to join in a larger fight that would benefit them as well. We need to organize our own people. We need to have a really deep conversation about fleeing the Midwest to organize outside our own communities because we think that's more radical. We have to think about the concessions we've been given by the powers that be and what it would take to do the deep work in our own communities and what that could yield." I'm put in mind of the iconoclastic White civil rights leader, the Rev. Will Campbell, who recently passed away. He was one of the only White pastors in the Southern Christian Leadership Conference (who coordinated the Montgomery bus boycott) in the early 1960s, and he had an epiphany that, to do the work of civil rights, he needed to be pastor to the Black Power leaders and also pastor to the Klan. He dedicated much of his ministry to building up solidarity within his own poor White Southern community with the broader civil rights movement.

Brooke shared, "There's a T-shirt that says, 'I believe in the revolutionary potential of my people.' What if that were true and we structured our organizing work accordingly?" I imagine that lawyer from the gospel story building up a community of "People at the Side of the Road" bearing witness to the humanity of their maligned Samaritan brothers, so that, together, the Jews and Samaritans could demand greater dignity from their real oppressors, the Roman Empire. I imagine lots of moments when some of their fellow Jews attacked them as Samaritan lovers or faith-traitors. I imagine some Samaritans telling them to mind their own business. But I imagine walls of division slowly crumbling, partly because the lawyer took Jesus' parable to heart and partly because he believed in his fellow Jews' capacity to embrace the same teachings about their common cause with Samaritans.

I still don't have a good answer for why some White people willingly wrestle with the issue of White privilege in the midst of the work they are doing. And I know that the costs of doing so are significant: lots of discomfort, instability, and the regular fear of saying or doing the wrong thing so that the people you love most feel compelled to let you know how you've let them down.

But for people like Brooke, Will Campbell, and my clergy friend from the Deep South, those costs are nothing compared to the cost of being isolated and separated from the gifts of their brothers and sisters. And, for people like them, the benefit is getting to be more fully who God made *them* to be.

I took Jonathan Kozol's advice and have been engaged in urban ministry for over eight years now. I carry class privilege and light skin privilege, and I've found that, most of the time, the people I get to work with don't care as long as I'm working for the community, privileging the voice of people who know what it's like to be poor and (more) brown. And my opinions and actions matter a lot, too. And when I don't realize that I'm making assumptions based on my class and skin privilege, I get checked, and we move on. And it feels better than not doing what I was called to do, or doing it in a way that doesn't fully honor the community that has lived and died for generations where I have called home for less than a decade.

Brooke's life is more complicated by paying attention to her privilege and being held accountable for it when she uses it unwittingly. But her life is richer because she grows every day closer to building the realm of God here on earth. And she has also built up the possibility of being both Samaritan and person at the side of the road at any given moment. And that constant openness to being either is where Brooke both experiences and creates Beloved Community.

CHAPTER QUESTIONS

1. What conversations have you heard about Native American named sports teams? What do you think about them? Have you heard the thoughts of Native Americans in your community? Why or why not?
2. Who is your neighbor in the story of the good Samaritan? (That is, who is from a different group than you whose help you might not expect?)
3. Were you surprised at any of the areas described as White Privilege? Are there any others you could add to the list?
4. Would you giving up a privilege help? Is that possible?
5. How can these privileges be spread to those without privilege? What would that look like on a community-wide level?
6. What does acknowledging White privilege have to do with the Beloved Community?

10

#Every28Hours

Dealing with the Grief of Racism in Real Time

I have worked hard throughout this book to share people's stories and share a little of my own perspective and biblical reflection in each chapter, but I have tried not to be aggressive, incendiary, or alienating to people who do not deal with race issues on a daily basis.

Every so often, however, an issue erupts that cuts deeply, and my filters go down. In August of 2014, Michael Brown was shot and killed by a police officer in Ferguson, Missouri. I was not going to write about it because there was so much already being written and my heart was too weighed down by the countless deaths of young Black men in this nation. But a friend said the church needed to hear from me. Since then, the facts of the moment have been debated ad nauseum, but it was the long line of deaths, each of which people tried to explain away, that really made me angry. I have chosen to place this chapter here because there is enough context for you to read it with a certain amount of grace now that we've been on a journey together, and I chose not to make it the last chapter, because I believe that the last chapters point to hope. We can't get to hope without acknowledging what's happening that robs us of our hope: despair is a necessary word, even though it is not the final word.

(Also, this is actually less angry and despairing than the post I wrote just after the non-indictment, which, if you are brave, can be found at http://sandhyajha.com/?p=783.) So here, unvarnished, is how I felt in the days immediately after the shooting, when I published a blog titled "Michael Brown, Worship This Sunday, and Confusing Unity with Comfort."[1]

I am tired of my church breaking my family's heart.

I wasn't going to write about Michael Brown. Many others have already done so, reflectively and powerfully, including writing about the role of the White church in the midst of this moment of pain.

I wasn't going to write about it because I've written on it before. And I've preached on it. And I've posted and I've tweeted and I've shouted at rallies for Alan Blueford[2] and Trayvon Martin[3] and Oscar Grant.[4]

I wasn't going to write about it because I wrote about it when the church didn't acknowledge Jordan Davis's murder[5] because…I don't know; Stand Your Ground fatigue? Lack of information? Complexity? Lack of relevance?

I wasn't going to write because if I wrote about Michael Brown, what would I do with the stories of John Crawford (killed in a Wal-Mart in southern Ohio for being seen in the toy aisle with a toy gun the store was selling) or Ezell Ford (shot by the LAPD while lying down) also pressing in on me? **But I am tired of the church breaking my family's heart.** And we have a chance to do something different this Sunday, if we don't sacrifice the lives of children on the altar of unity yet again.

---

[1]Originally posted at http://sandhyajha.com/2014/08/michael-brown-worship-this-sunday-and-confusing-unity-with-comfort/.

[2]An unarmed eighteen-year-old Black man shot in the back and killed by an Oakland police officer in May 2012.

[3]An unarmed seventeen-year-old Black youth shot and killed by a twenty-eight-year-old man who felt threatened by Martin in Martin's own neighborhood in Sanford, Florida, in February 2012.

[4]An unarmed twenty-two-year-old Black man shot and killed by a Bay Area Rapid Transit officer in Oakland on New Year's Day 2009.

[5]An unarmed seventeen-year-old Black youth shot and killed in his car at a gas station by a man who approached his car and said he felt threatened by the music Davis and his friends were playing in Jacksonville, Florida, in November 2012. I wrote about this at http://sandhyajha.com/?p=507

One of my best friends goes to a multi-racial church. She's African American. She's raising an African American son and daughter. And she believes in a Christ who unites us. So at some cost to her culturally and for the sake of her children having worship that moves them, she worships at a church that has excellent worship and children's programming and both Black and White men in leadership. (Yeah—that's another issue…)

During prayer time on February 16 of this year, my friend didn't hear people lifting up the name of Jordan Davis. There was no ritual to acknowledge the continued failure of the criminal justice system in America. The fact was not grieved that Jordan Davis's murderer is now leading a movement telling White people to "Stand Their Ground" whenever they see a Black man because Black men are always threatening. My friend intentionally worships at a church focused on unity.

And my friend's church broke her heart because unity is almost always unconsciously driven by the dominant culture's lived experience and very rarely by an awareness that acts of injustice against some communities do not happen in isolation but as part of a pattern.

I am tired of the church breaking my family's heart. **I am tired of the church unconsciously and unintentionally choosing unity, but really choosing comfort.**

I am tired of the church unconsciously choosing comfort in the face of the tragedy that should be breaking all of our hearts: **every twenty-eight hours, a Black man is killed by police[6] in the United States.** Black men who are our sons and brothers and nephews, because we chose to be a part of a faith that says we are one in the Spirit, that we are one family. We worship a God whose son was killed unjustly by the authorities for no justifiable reason, and we denigrate the religious leaders of the time for making up disgusting justifications for why he needed to die.

And I hear people saying that this is complicated. And I hear them saying that we need more facts. And I hear them saying that the protests in response are unacceptable and

---

[6]Or vigilantes.

so we should not look like we are condoning violence by agreeing with what drove people to violence. And I hear that law enforcement has a hard job. I definitely hear that when we talk about this, we ignore Black-on-Black violence. And I even occasionally hear that "his appearance made him a target." *And I think of the crucifixion.* And I think about religious leaders desiring unity. And I think about how many members of the body of Christ is "an acceptable loss" so that we don't have to speak out.

I've been told that this prophetic ministry comes more easily to me because I'm political and have only shared this type of message in churches that are open to political messages.

But a prophetic message isn't political. A prophetic message says, "God is grieving because this world is out of alignment with God's will." **A prophetic message is saturated in tears and grief because real people are being harmed and God's community is ignoring that fact.** Jeremiah and Amos and Micah were not politicians; *they were professional mourners.*

And our desire to avoid grief—God's grief, our family grief—is placing us in a dangerous position of also avoiding God's call.

We are not being asked to be political. We are being asked to be faithful. When our family members' hearts are breaking, our job is to mourn with them, to understand why they are mourning, to find paths of healing and reconciliation and—yes—justice. All we are being asked to do this Sunday is to grieve. All we are being asked to do beyond this Sunday is to explore why this happens repeatedly (#every28hours) instead of explaining away every single instance.

There are lots of reasons not to know about this. We don't have conversation partners. We don't have lived experience. We don't know about microaggressions and disparate sentencing based on race and how race actually shapes fear responses in dangerous ways and the fact that four-year-old Black boys are learning to fear the police instead of trusting them.

Another friend texted me that he was watching CNN with his mixed-race son, who said, "There's no way that Missouri cop will get away with shooting that Black teen," and then, "That just looks like a protest. Why are they calling it a riot?"

My friend and his son will mourn, and they will discuss the pattern of injustice that devastates people from one race far more than another. That conversation will be uncomfortable, but it is necessary to create the kind of unity my friend dreams of, one that involves justice and equality as well as diversity. They are not religious, but I wish I knew that, if they went to church, they would be able to do the same thing in a loving and supportive community.

I do not have to raise a son who has to be trained in how to reduce police officers' anxiety, and I do not have to figure out how to explain to him that this still will not guarantee his safety. But I am part of the body of Christ with people who do. And if I don't try to understand that experience, I'm not actually being part of the family. If I don't mourn this loss with the rest of my family, I'm not being part of the family. If I claim that it is disruptive or trouble making or undermining of church unity, then I am participating in breaking my family's heart.

Because grieving the untimely death of an innocent young man and thousands more like him over the years is not disuniting. It is discomforting. And we can no longer choose comfort built on the dead bodies of the innocent.

11

"But I Don't Think of You As..."

Navigating Mixed Race Identity in a One-or-the-other World

> *"I'm lucky because I have so many clashing cultural, racial things going on: black, Jewish, Irish, Portuguese, Cherokee. I can float and be part of any community I want. The thing is, I do identify with being black, and if people don't identify me that way, that's their issue. I'm happy to challenge people's understanding of what it looks like to be biracial, because guess what? In the next 50 years, people will start looking more and more like me."*
>
> —Rashida Jones[1]

There's something about growing up in a little town. It's like the line from the theme song of that old TV show *Cheers*: Everybody knows your name. Now, kids fight sometimes, and when they do, they resort to whatever hurts. In Vinita, Oklahoma, that's when Yuki (then known as Barbara) would get called Jap or Nip or when the kids would pull the skin

---

[1]Brantley Bardin, "Meet Karen from The Office: Interview with Rashida Jones," *Women's Health Magazine,* March 5, 2008. Available at: http://www.womenshealthmag.com/rashida-jones-interview?fullpage=1

back at their temples to make slant eyes. And that hurt, but it was mixed in with her being part of a large, German-American family who made up a large chunk of the town's population and had lived there for more than half a century, so it wasn't constant.

Yuki is the daughter of a Japanese woman and a White American sailor. Her parents' plan after marriage had been for her dad to retire from the Navy and for them to move to the West Coast, rather than stay in Japan to face the racism and prejudice that Yuki's mom was sure her mixed-race children would experience there. "I wanted you to grow up in America where there's no racism," she explained to her daughter. But six months before Yuki was born, her father died from a sudden illness, and her mother and two small children were able to move to his hometown in rural Oklahoma within days after his death.

College was when she started getting the question, "Where are you from? No, where are you *really* from?" that mixed-race people (and people who clearly have Asian heritage) get so frequently. In the world outside Vinita, she wasn't "Frank Schwartz's daughter," and other people were trying to figure out who (and what) she was.

As a journalist in Muskogee, Yuki (still Barbara at this point) received a crash course in what solidarity looked like and where she might be invited into it as a mixed-race person in a mostly Black-and-White context. Oklahoma has a long history of Black-White racism, at one time being an area with the most lynchings of Black people *per capita* of any place in the nation, along with a legacy of Native-White racism in relation to the multiple Indigenous people living there. Decades after that terrible era, racial tensions had quieted but still lurked beneath the societal surface, erupting in social, economic, and political incidents. Yuki began meeting people on both sides of visceral Black-White tensions. "I was between this Black and White division," she said, "and I found myself standing with the Black community most often, because I was welcomed, because I was trusted, because I was one of the non-White reporters. And also, I think, because I listened and I learned that what was going on was wrong." She felt those stories deeply and resonated with the injustice of their experience, and she knew that they were reaching out to her out of solidarity—in Oklahoma, they knew she would have experienced some of the challenges of not being completely White.

Yet, at the same time, she notes, "I was disavowing the race thing, because, 'Why can't we all just get along?'" she said, quoting Rodney King. She was dying her hair and wearing green contact lenses and not necessarily thinking she was trying to blend in with White culture. This reaction may have emerged from an important lesson Yuki picked up in high school. One Halloween night, students from her school came to her house and shoe-polished "JAP GO HOME" on the windows of the house and her car. They didn't know the history of Japanese internment camps in the United States. They didn't know what it meant to be considered a foreigner even though this was the only country, the only town you had ever known. They just knew it would garner a reaction. And while it was awful, what was more awful was her band director explaining to her that she needed to forgive them, because they didn't *mean* to hurt her that much. What she realized in that moment, when an authority figure told her that her feelings mattered less than the lack of particularly malicious intent by her schoolmates, was that "there was always going to be a space—an uncontrollable space—between me and the people who made up my day-to-day life because I didn't know what was going to evoke that sudden reaction from someone who in all other ways was a friend." The temptation not to bring attention to one's difference is pretty understandable.

In the early 2000s, Yuki (still Barbara) moved to Oklahoma City and eventually went back to school, getting a degree in religious studies. During this time, she studied liberation theology[2] and came across a book written by Asian American

---

[2]*Liberation theology* is the study of God with the understanding that God is on the side of the oppressed, and that the voice of oppressed people's

theologians. They engaged the question "Where are you from?" as a theological question. "I cried when I read that book," she says. She realized she wasn't the only one dealing with the issue of identity. "I read it and thought, 'I'm not crazy! I'm not making this up!'" Engaging liberation theology helped Yuki claim her Asian American identity.

Yuki and I know each other through a group of Asian feminist theologians. It is, as you can imagine, a pretty small bunch of folks, and I naturally gravitated toward the woman who was mixed and definitely claimed her racial-ethnic identity instead of ignoring it and trying to "pass" for White. I wanted to know if she had navigated her life as I had navigated mine.

I hear a lot of my own experiences in the story of Yuki, and there are also some differences. I don't remember too many moments of being mocked for my racial background. It was a source of puzzlement to some, and I have evangelical friends who continue to pray for my Hindu father's soul, but we never had a cross burned on our lawn or property damaged in this country. I'm light skinned, and, despite my name, as long as I acted like the other kids in school, there were enough other things to pick on that they never resorted to that one. (I remember four other kids of color in my class of 200, two of whom were mixed as well, and, as far as I know, that was true for all of us.) And that's what we did—we may have had unusual customs at home and hung out with people from different cultures on the weekend, but we were regular all-American kids at school.

I became a little more aware of my racial identity when I moved to a school in the Chicago suburbs with Asian American students who had the same experiences as me, but would joke about them with each other in class and incorporate them into their reflections for essays. It made them "other," but it gave them a community. They didn't have to worry about being American enough because they weren't trying to be. They were my heroes.

Things were different, though, when my family moved back to Akron, and this time I talked about race and talked about my racial identity. I remember one of my beloved mentors saying to me, "I miss how, before you moved, you were just Sandhya." The thing is, I know a lot of mixed-race people and people of color in general who function in their community as just themselves as individuals. That definitely feels better for the people around them, and it very possibly feels better for them. It creates the feeling (which may be true) that this person's race doesn't matter. In fact, my mentor said it to me because she was aware that by not being "just Sandhya," I was creating a distance that hadn't been there, and I think she really worried I would be isolated from all of the people around me who were just themselves.

So why don't I just want to be "just Sandhya"? Why doesn't Yuki want to be "just Yuki"? (Or, actually, Why doesn't she want to be "just Barbara"?)

For me, Esther is one of the most resonant books in the Bible. It's a complicated book soaked with revenge by the oppressed that feels a little bit like the second half of Quentin Tarantino's *Kill Bill*, but that notwithstanding, it's a story about a people surviving as a minority. Let's start with Haman. Talk about a nasty piece of work, that guy. Since Mordecai, a Jew, won't bow down to the Persian king (God's insistence that Jews not worship anyone but God got them in a lot of trouble over the millennia), he gets on Haman's bad side and Haman decides to wipe out the entire Israeli people as a result. But the king had unwittingly married a Jewish woman, Esther. She had kept her identity under wraps, given that the Jewish people were not the most popular race in the Persian Empire. So when Mordecai learns of the plot, he goes to his identity-hiding niece Esther and tells her to advocate for her people. When she says it is a capital offense to go to the king unbidden, he famously responds, "Do not think that in the king's palace you will escape any more than all the other Jews. For if you keep silence at such a time as this, relief and deliverance will rise for the Jews from another quarter, but you and your father's family will perish. Who knows? Perhaps you have come to royal dignity for just such a time as this" (4:13–14, NRSV).

I definitely sit in conversations during which people forget that I'm a person of color and I hear things that other people of color don't hear. And I get the sometimes exhausting privilege of reframing the conversation. I get to participate in conversations in which first-generation immigrants who are my community; and poor people who are my community; and Muslims, Sikhs, and Hindus who are my community do not get to participate. Part of why I claim my South Asian identity so publicly is so that when I hear someone say, "But I don't think of you as Asian," I can make a little joke, such as, "Oh! I made the cut?" that hopefully reminds them that the implicit race hierarchy that's been imposed on all of us isn't necessarily true; it's not necessarily better to be White than Asian or anything else. Like Esther, I can pass. Like Esther, I recognize God's place on the margins and want to use my place at both the center and the margins to forward God's work in the world.

I remember talking one time with a friend who is half Black and half White, and who will never be able to pass even though he has a mixed-race identity not too different from mine. "I didn't ask for this privilege," I complained in relation to yet another conversation in which I had to remind a group of people that using the phrase "those people" in reference to immigrants was unhelpful in either building relationship or creating effective policy. "Maybe God gave you that privilege for a reason," my friend said. "God gave it to you to so you could work to eliminate privilege in general." (Yeah, my friends are grandiose like that. It comes from reading the Bible too much.)

Now I want to be clear on one thing: mixed-race people navigate their racial identity in a million different ways. I know another Scottish-Indian couple (my parents aren't the only ones) who have three adult children. One uses a Western name and his primary identity is as a DJ. He's never visited India. One has visited once or twice and uses her Indian name but is pretty enmeshed in a White community, married to a White husband, raising her kids with very little cultural identity beyond the dominant Anglo culture. The third is militant and hardcore and visits India and is plugged into the South Asian activist community. Their mother isn't sure why they turned out that way since she raised them all the same, and she was interested that I had turned out the way I did.

America still works on a binary a lot of the time: you are "either/or." However, there are more and more of us mixed-race kids in the country, and we push against that binary model (or accept it) in lots of different ways. Some just want to be like everyone else (which is actually more about blending into the dominant culture). Some don't want to choose (which is why the Census now lets you tick off multiple boxes). And some feel like being "Hapa" (the Hawaiian term for mixed race, particularly popular among Asian-White mixed race people) *is* their racial identity. Yuki and I aren't total outliers by emphasizing our minority identity foremost, but we're certainly not the only way mixed-race people make sense of their identity.

Race has been constructed differently for various races in this country. It's a weird, cobbled together hodgepodge of unwritten rules oriented toward preserving power for a very small group of people. As a result, when President Obama was elected, I received dozens of texts from friends and colleagues and from young people I worked with on the day of his inauguration celebrating the first Black President. A young woman who was half Black and half White, and who wants to claim both parts of that identity, texted me: "Our First Black President!!!"

I texted her back, "And our First Hapa President!"

"Huh?"

After I explained Hapa, I texted, "So he's your people BOTH ways!" Even though this young woman wants both parts of her to be acknowledged, the primary identity imposed on her is Black. She hadn't even thought about the fact that the President was, like her, biracial. And in a country founded on anti-Blackness and White Supremacy, where the rest of us settle into our position somewhere in between, it is not surprising that President Obama and she don't get to play the biracial card in the same way that Yuki and I could.

In a binary world, with light skin (and red hair, thanks to the ancient Indian dying technique of henna), the primary identity externally imposed on me is White. I have a friend or two who think I claim my racial identity to "exceptionalize" myself, to make myself special, or to claim some sort of oppression I don't actually experience. Truth be told, my life is *way* easier because I have light skin than it would be otherwise. I also come from a community that does get stereotyped and bears burdens, but also benefits from not being Black in a country founded (as I said before) on anti-Blackness.

So I try to clearly name my mixed-race status and my privilege. And I also talk about the community I come from: a community of immigrants, a community of freedom fighters, a community of people who are only welcomed insofar as they follow the rules of society as it currently exists. (And isn't that true for all of us in some fashion?)

Yuki says she doesn't get the question, "Where are you from?" any more, "Maybe because the progressives I hang out with now don't ask that question." Part of the reason the name "Barbara" became "Yuki" is that Yuki now understands identity as not only being cultural and social but also political. "What I learned in Muskogee as I was first learning about race and racism in the U.S. was that our identity is also about our solidarities. So I choose to be Yuki because for me that's part of the struggle to end racism. And that's a choice I got to make as a mixed person. And I'm glad I made it." Her name signifies her identity and also helps people make the connection to her cultural heritage. So instead of, "Where are you from?" people instead ask, "Where's that name from?" And perhaps in that moment of dialogue, Yuki can contribute to wisdom and dignity for a community that has not always experienced those things. In that moment of privilege and solidarity, Yuki becomes Esther and, in our response to her story, we all get to be a part of the Beloved Community God intends.

CHAPTER QUESTIONS

1. Why do children pick on each other? Do racial insults hurt more? Why or why not? Using the definition of racism=race prejudice + power, what do children learn about systems from racial insults in the world around them?
2. Have you ever had to stand up for what was right even though people weren't expecting you to? What was it like?
3. Have you thought of the story of Esther this way before? How does it make you reflect on Scripture differently when you think about Israelites as a mistreated racial minority?
4. Do you know any mixed-race people? How do they navigate their identities? How is that shaped by how other people define them? Is there a "right way" to be mixed race? Does the particular mixture affect how a person is allowed to self-define?
5. What does claiming a racial identity have to do with the Beloved Community?

12

Oppression Olympics, Intersectional Faith, and the Integrated Self

"I consider myself West African, among other cultural identities, and a writer, among other creative ones."

—Taiye Salasi

"Never be bullied into silence. Never allow yourself to be made a victim. Accept no one's definition of your life, but define yourself."

—Harvey Fierstein

"So God created humanity in God's own image, in the image of God God created humanity; male and female God created them."

—Genesis 1:27

Emerson[1] once had a Scottish boyfriend. Emerson's Scottish boyfriend once said to him, "You have a Negro smile." If I had a Scottish boyfriend who said that to me, I

[1]Not his real name.

might have punched him, but Emerson knew the guy well enough to ask, "What do you mean by that?"

In film school in Edinburgh, the boyfriend explained that their film instructor showed them movies with caricatured subservient Black people in them. The Black people would smile big, toothy grins, but the instructor encouraged his students to notice the fury bubbling invisible below the surface of that smile. "If you were a slave," Emerson's boyfriend commented, "you wouldn't revolt; you would just smile and then poison your master when he wasn't looking."

Emerson looked at him for a moment and then acknowledged that sounded about right.

My friend Emerson shatters more stereotypes per minute than seems possible, and he takes some small pleasure, I think, in using the resulting confusion to shatter even more. If a person is startled that he's such an articulate African American man, they'll be shocked that his Ph.D. focuses on the European Reformation instead of Black liberation theology. People who can relate to that won't expect him to have been shaped in childhood by the image of tanks rolling down his street in Cleveland in the late 1960s, or that his ministry today is informed by his parents having to use food stamps, or how the Black Power movement runs deep in his Presbyterian veins. If they know all that, they might not expect his partner to be Asian American. Nor will they necessarily expect him to have a deep understanding of mental health issues from a brilliant and schizophrenic mother. And if a person makes sense of all of that, the role of his sexual orientation may or may not fit in with any of the above information.

Part of the reason I wanted to chat with Emerson for this book is that, in some ways, he embodies that fancy word "intersectionality." There are two reasons I care about that fancy word. One is that, whenever I talk about race, inevitably someone will say, "But I'm a woman [or I'm gay or I grew up poor] so I experience life on the margins and therefore am not responsible for systemic racism." And it's true that our world is more complicated than victims and oppressors based on any one issue. However, we often use that truth to avoid dealing with hard issues such as race. It's what an anti-racism trainer I know calls "The Oppression Olympics." Sometimes, because I'm a woman, I believe that means I couldn't hurt someone based on their race. I might even feel the need to prove that *my* oppression is worse than theirs. It can become almost a competitive sport. "Oh, yeah? Well, what about *this* major form of oppression?" (We saw a lot of this in the arguments between Hillary Clinton and Barack Obama supporters in 2008—Which was worse, sexism or racism?)

So intersectionality helps me think through those distinctions of where I'm on the margins and where I benefit from privilege on multiple fronts at the same time. Second, my role in any conversation about race is profoundly shaped by my own intersectional location.

If you meet a middle class academic, you might not realize he had poor roots. A Black person deals with stereotypes being imposed on him that people don't even realize they harbor. A man who recently married his male partner of fourteen years is embraced by some and rejected by others, most of whom won't know that his ex-wife asked to attend the wedding. And all of those things are Emerson and define how Emerson gets treated. Emerson lives at the intersection of multiple identities that he does not have complete control over. Each of those identities shape how people perceive him, including people from any of his own communities, and the mixture of those identities impacts in complex ways how people "read" him.

The same is true of a straight White man—he also lives at the intersection of multiple identities that he does not have complete control over, and each of those identities shape how people perceive him. It's just that each of those identities are considered to be "normative" in our society, so he might not notice what's being imposed on him.

That's intersectionality. Society teaches us who people of other races are. Society teaches us who people are based on gender. Society teaches us who gay people are (and implicitly who straight people are). We don't mean to treat people differently based on any of those things, but no matter how well meaning, we often unintentionally and subconsciously make assumptions about people we see from certain groups either based on what we see or what we learn. But what happens when those different definitions of who we are intersect with each other (a Black gay middle class clergy man, for example)?

I think about this more than a lot of people because I live at some funny intersections that make me awkward to categorize. People do it all the time. They just each categorize me differently and then get frustrated if I don't fit into the category they personally constructed for me. I'm a light-skinned, mixed-race woman (or at least light skinned for the name attached to me) whose first language is English but whose community of accountability in the church is primarily non-native-English speaking Asian and Pacific Islanders. I'm heterosexual and not-yet middle aged. I have no immediately obvious disabilities. That means people engage me in different ways depending on how much of my identity they know and how much dissonance my identity creates for them. I get a lot of privilege in certain circles and my voice is less valued in others, partly for reasons of gender or race or orientation or ability or education, partly because of the funny soup of some or all of those things. I think about my privilege (and occasional lack of privilege) more than is probably healthy, because taking that privilege for granted harms others in my community of accountability and ignoring the marginalization means it goes unaddressed. And as a result sometimes I sound shrill and hypersensitive even to myself.

Intersectionality isn't the end of the story, though, as Emerson is quick to point out. As important as it is in understanding our current situation, it is not a solution to a problem; it is simply a way of naming a problem that doesn't usually get named. Once, he was sitting in a room with a new high-ranking clergy colleague in his Presbytery who casually tossed off the comment, "I think for the church to provide holy unions covers the issue of gay marriage well enough to avoid controversy, don't you?" Emerson said, "Well, the church had nothing to do with weddings for the first 1,000 years." When the high-ranking clergy colleague said he didn't find the historic argument compelling, Emerson responded, "Don't ever say something like that to a church history scholar."

This obviously threw his colleague for a bit of a loop, but not as much as when Emerson subtly mentioned that since his relationship with his partner embodied for better or worse, in sickness and in health, he wasn't clear on why that wasn't a marriage in the sight of God or the church. It was an intersectional moment that snuck up on Emerson's colleague who had decided who Emerson was based on three visible qualities: Black, male, and clergy. And Emerson smiled, and he didn't exactly poison his colleague's soup, but he named some uncomfortable truths while seeming incredibly civil. Emerson was aware of this intersectional moment, and how he responded was by simply being his fully integrated self. He didn't hide any part of who he was or lead with any part of who he was; he just brought all of himself into the conversation in ways that made transparent the assumptions of his colleague.

Emerson's colleague was later recognized for coming out strongly in favor of gay marriage in the Presbyterian Church. Maybe a conversation with someone much more complex than he was expecting had some influence on that shift.

For the high-ranking clergy colleague, Emerson's Blackness hid his gayness. Emerson was treated a certain way as a Black man and then this colleague shifted the way he engaged Emerson upon learning he was educated and then that he was gay; the categories layered on each other in ways hard to parse out. For others, though, his status as gay clergy with a Ph.D. hides the upbringing that shaped him, making him markedly more militant on issues of race and class than most people expect.

Another example of intersectionality in Emerson's life is that when he sought ordination in a Presbytery rumored to be somewhat racist, he didn't have any initial allies in his mostly White denomination until "the gay mafia," as he jokingly calls the well-organized gay clergy and laity in that Presbytery, learned that he was "one of them," at which point they fought for him tooth and nail. Not necessarily before they learned he was gay, but as soon as they learned that fact.

Often in my anti-racism work, this messy matrix is just one bridge too far. "This is the *problem,*" my loving and progressive colleagues wail. "We should treat each other as *people.*"

Yes. Yes, we should. And Emerson's way of being in the world is exactly that—he doesn't wear just one hat as the occasion calls for. I remember an e-mail he once sent me that started out with a phrase in Latin and ended with a quote from Tyler Perry's Madea. It's true that what matters most about us is what is on the inside. We should just be people.

Yet I know that when I saw a woman on the street today in a hijab (headscarf) and a black dress that touched the ground and went to her wrists standing with her boyfriend who was wearing shorts and a T-shirt, I had an immediate narrative that layered her religion on top of her gender in how I understood her role in her family and in society and also her self-perception. I am really ashamed of that fact, but I know that living in post-9/11 America, being shaped by Western feminism, and a healthy dose of Hindu (and Indian Christian) anti-Muslim bias has shaped my subconscious. So, in a split second, I saw a woman whose body is considered a source of temptation for men and is obligated to hide it while the man with her could dress however made him comfortable in the hot sun. "Her religion and her gender oppressed her," was my snap narrative. It is only because I have cultivated friendships with a diverse array of Muslim women over my life that I notice the assumptions I am making and know they are just that: assumptions that may or may not be true in this particular situation.[2]

---

[2]Like many non-Muslims shaped by Western culture, I always thought of hijab (headscarves worn by Muslim women) as oppressive and sexist, and burka (a loose dress covering almost every inch of a woman) as doubly so. Then I talked with a Muslim feminist friend of mine, who doesn't wear a headscarf, about the period of her life when she did. She was so tired of the constant judgment and objectification she faced in high school, where men seemed to think it was their right to evaluate her, that she wore a hijab as a way of saying to them, "You don't get to do that. I am forcing you to engage with me on intellectual grounds, not just because you think I'm pretty enough to talk to or sexy enough to make lewd comments to." If I had seen my friend in high school in a hijab, that would not have been the narrative I created for her.

And I also see the gears shifting in the brains of people I meet for the first time when I do congregational transformation consultations after they have seen my name in print as their assigned consultant; the confusion and relief and reshuffling of the deck of how they thought our time together would look. Sometimes I can tell they're reshuffling when they say, "Sorry, what are you here for? Ah, okay. You're... how do you say that?" and then pointedly introduce me to the pastor, "This is, how do you say it again? She's here for the congregational assessment." One time a Regional Minister flat out said, "Well, you're not who I was expecting. Where's that name from? Huh? You don't look Indian. Okay, then." That almost audible reshuffling is about the layers of assumptions about the puzzle pieces of my identity and how the world makes sense of my culture and gender and presenting appearance.

And last of all, I see how straight White men in a clergy gathering assume they will be listened to (and are), and how that differs from how Asian-Pacific female clergy are heard or feel the right to have their own voice. The same goes for Latino men, or gay White male clergy or gay male clergy of color. I notice how that shifts and doesn't shift depending on the makeup of people in the room, and how it gets discussed or doesn't.

I agree: simply naming intersectionality, as I mentioned before, is not the solution. Intersectionality in and of itself can end up being a limiting factor; it can constrain us to certain boxes. Intersectionality may acknowledge more boxes, but they are still boxes. Growing up in an all-Black neighborhood for Emerson meant that there was a huge breadth to what it meant to be Black, so it was okay for him to listen to classical music and not be less Black. Stopping at intersectionality, Emerson cautions, runs the risk of narrowing what it means to claim any part of your identity. At the same time, pretending the boxes aren't there stops us from seeing where unconscious assumptions limit our imagination about one another and about ourselves.

The hard work of both acknowledging and overcoming multiple oppressions (and multiple privileges), I believe, involves the willingness to embrace all of those parts of ourselves at the same time. That's a long journey that doesn't happen all at once. It's something all of us can work on, and it's something that will look different for every single one of us. I've often been invited to represent the Asian American community. When I walk into any of those meetings, I might be shy to raise women's issues because that's not why I was invited. But that's where I'm letting myself be compartmentalized instead of bringing my whole self into the room. And truth be told, I am better for having other people bring their whole selves into the room. I can think of times friends in a meeting on immigration issues have reminded me about gender issues I was ignoring, because they brought their whole selves into the room as well.

For Emerson, this isn't just an "it works better this way" issue. It's a theological issue. We preach the unity of Christ a lot in the church, and then we only bring part of ourselves to the table. Sometimes we withhold for fear of being judged, by the dominant culture but also by our own culture if we're non-White. Emerson describes listening to classical LPs in his home in high school, in a community where Black was the norm, so there were many ways of being Black. When he went to college in the 1970s, he was thrilled that he'd find more intellectuals who shared his love of the classics and was heartbroken to discover that, in a predominantly White college, Black was more narrowly defined and therefore his love of "White music" was deemed suspect. In the realm of God, Emerson puts forth, the love of classical music is not the sole realm of White people. These multiple identities we carry as intersectional people do not all have to be lived in identical ways, and that, Emerson might say, is what makes them beautiful and God-given. And more glorious, he would argue, is simply to be us.

I'm a little more hesitant to talk about the simply being us stuff because I think it is a seductive place for us to move too quickly without having wrestled with the impacts of oppression that still function today. While simply being us, we need to be aware that other people only see (or want to see) parts of us. And we need to be able to name those things, in order to build up the realm of God. And yet, as I said, I have a lot more fun with friends who aren't just a particular part of themselves but are their whole hip hop loving, classical music trained, architecture obsessed, housing rights selves, for example. Or their family loving, dog obsessed, political junkie, guitar playing, immigrant selves. Or whatever amazing combination of traits has evolved in us.

I will confess that there is little love lost between the apostle Paul and me. But here was a guy who lived in a seriously intersectional space, aspects of which he was painfully aware and others of which he was blissfully unaware. As a result, he used his Jewish heritage to his advantage and sometimes realized the cost of that identity in the Roman Empire (or did the ancient equivalent of "code switching" to his Roman citizenship when advantageous to his cause). He knew the world that was open to him as a Greek-speaking member of the merchants' guild, but that he needed to own his Jewish identity so that he neither set himself up to be exposed to potential Greek followers for pretending to be something he wasn't nor alienated his Jewish brothers and sisters by denying them, which is one of the unintentional injuries we cause when we "pass." He didn't realize that his voice had a different impact as a man or that this was a problem, and while he lifted up specific women in church leadership, his statements about women in general implied the individual women he knew were exceptions rather than the rule. Paul had a physical disability or ailment of some sort that clearly evoked compassion and care from some new Christians but also caused him to reflect on infirmity in unusual ways for someone who otherwise knew power. For example, he reflects on this injury in the following way in 2 Corinthians 12:8–10: "Three times I appealed to the Lord about this, that it would leave me, but he said to me, 'My grace is sufficient for you, for power is made perfect in weakness.' So I will boast all the more gladly of my weaknesses, so that the power of Christ may dwell in me. Therefore I am content with weaknesses, insults, hardships, persecutions, and calamities for the sake of Christ; for whenever I am weak, then I am strong" (NRSV).

Paul chooses to claim what society would call a weakness, and for which he experiences discrimination, as a way of connecting to God and claiming as core to his spiritual identity. Paul was a man shaped by his culture, and that's what intersectionality is all about: it is about the multiple ways we are perceived based on what others know about us.

I sometimes wonder what Christianity would look like today if Paul were more aware of his intersectional identity, of the ways that privilege in certain areas and marginalization in other areas shaped his voice and impact, even when he acknowledged that not all of his words were God-ordained. I witness Emerson advocating for women in a non-paternalistic way when his voice as a male and even as a Black male will be heard more loudly. I witness him recognizing his spaces of relative privilege and empathizing with others from his spaces of relative marginalization. After I wrote a blog post in April 2012 about the hate crime murder of Muslim immigrant Shaima Alawadi and the nonresponse of progressive Christians who protested hate crimes against young Black men, I remember Emerson sending me the tear-inducing manuscript of his Good Friday sermon eulogizing her as he grieved the murder of Jesus Christ at the hands of the Roman authorities. And I wonder if an intersectionally aware Paul, a more fully integrated Paul, would have looked a little bit like Emerson.

Emerson's Black Baptist great uncle was a preacher in the Jim Crow South. Emerson and I talked about a lot of things as I interviewed him for this chapter. And after our second meeting, he shared this story that I want to offer as an illustration of the integrated Christian contributing to the Beloved Community where we are all our integrated selves. "After discussing the power of being in the presence of God's majesty, in whose presence there is no intersectionality, I recalled my favorite part of the church service as a boy (besides Holy Communion). It was when my great uncle would raise his right hand at the conclusion of the service, the sleeves of his impeccable Geneva gown billowing at his wrists, and paraphrase Jude: 'Now unto him who is able to keep you from falling, and to present you faultless before the presence of his glory with exceeding joy: to the only wise God our Savior, be power, glory, dominion, and majesty, henceforth now and forevermore...(Choral threefold Amen.)'"

CHAPTER QUESTIONS

1. What does your intersectional map look like? What combinations give you privilege or marginalize you? Have you noticed this before? Why or why not?
2. Have you found it difficult to "just be your integrated self" when people are trying to impose other identities on you? How have you navigated that? Does it get easier?
3. Do you think of people from certain racial groups as being similar to each other? How might that limit their ability to be their fully integrated selves? Has that happened to you? How was it limiting?
4. What does reflecting on intersectionality have to do with the Beloved Community?

Conclusion

Beloved Communities

On a Monday night in February, I sat down with a group of people to see if we might have a Beloved Community in us.

The gathered community was made up of a teacher's aide, a hospital chaplain, a community organizer, a book store clerk, a self-employed home cleaner, a sex workers' rights activist, an after school program director, and a roller derby queen. Alternately categorized, we were three hip hop artists, a poet, a spoken word artist, two painters, and two writers. We were Black, Latin@, Asian / Hapa, Indigenous, and White.

Part of why we gathered was my former co-pastor's and my dream to build a spiritual community grounded in socially conscious hip hop. That dream emerged from our experiences with young people in our community who we can tell are deeply spiritual but will probably never set foot in a church. That dream has become more important to us as we struggle to find any place our spiritual selves really belong. Why everyone else showed up, I'm still trying to figure out. But it was still pretty great.

No one at the table of ten knew more than three other people well. And that didn't stop us from going deep fast. We talked about what it meant to grow up in certain neighborhoods. We talked about what it meant to grow up in religious communities where there are "right answers" and "wrong answers." We talked about what it meant to grow up with elders (and about the difference between elders and people who happen to be old). We talked about what it means to lose friends and family to violence. All of this under the auspices of forming a leadership team for a conscious hip hop group.

I'm going to have to figure out how to deal with Asian-Black tensions in Oakland in a whole different way as not-pastor in a conscious hip hop gathering that talks about issues that matter, especially as an Asian middle-class person in a group that is intentionally predominantly Black and working class. I'm going to have to learn a lot of humility so that other voices carry weight. In other words I'm going to have to learn to shut up and listen.

When I talked with Tai Amri about getting this started after several years of thinking about it, it was by text. "I don't know about you," I texted him about six months after we had left First Christian Church of Oakland, "but I need the Ubuntu Community in my life now."

The Ubuntu Community. That's what we're calling it. The Swahili word that loosely translates to "I am because we are," which played a key role in the vision of South Africa's Truth and Reconciliation Commission to deal honestly with the legacy of racism in South Africa so the country could move forward.

I'm taking a break from traditional church right now. I often work with churches that are so battered and bruised that all they can do is focus on what is right in front of them. They worry more about holding on to the building than in reaching out to the community. They worry more about getting members to boost their dwindling coffers than in nurturing people into a deep relationship with Christ. They worry more about getting people to make the pies for the annual sale (and making apple pies exactly the way the previous generations made them: "Here, you're doing it wrong, just let me do it instead") than learning what the people moving into their neighborhood like to eat.

And while I see race and culture as critical spiritual issues, many of the churches I work with are far too overwhelmed with survival to realize that learning to engage in incredibly vulnerable conversations about race could help them be oases of healing in a world of brokenness. They do not by and large realize that loving your neighbor—your different race and different worldview and different class and different nationality and different orientation and different religion neighbor—can save your soul, and it can save your congregation.

I'm also taking a break from traditional church because so many of the young people I work with in Oakland are deeply spiritual, but they don't have a place to wrestle with challenging questions of faith without someone trying to point them to the "right" answer. This is even more true for people of color, and there are few places where they can be their whole cultural selves and their whole spiritual selves in all of their complexity. This has felt particularly true in our community as young people of color take to the streets in grief and rage over the repeated absolution of the (unrepented of) sin of police brutality toward young Black people, with timid, pedantic, or uneven presence from the faith community at a crystallizing moment. So we're building up a leadership team of people of color (with one White ally that Tai Amri invited because of her deep investment in the Native American community) who are spiritual seekers together.

It's sometimes hard for me to admit I'm stepping away from formal leadership within institutional church because I feel so ungrateful, but I've hit a wall in my work to help the church become the space these particular young people need. I've kind of hit a wall in my work to help the church become the space that I need, too.

So I gather with "like-hearted people," as a friend of mine says, and do my best to start building up the Beloved Community here in Oakland.

At the same time, I find myself thinking of other beloved communities. They may not connect with my particular spiritual needs, but they remind me that I'm not alone in this pursuit:

- The lay-led Church of the Savior in Washington, D.C., which requires members to be in covenant around spiritual practice and servant leadership and community support and accountability, with a particular focus on economic justice issues and cultivating leadership and discipleship among the city's poor.

- City of Refuge United Church of Christ, which nurtures up leadership from every corner—homeless, queer[1] or transgender, Black or Brown or White, formerly incarcerated, or any combination of the above—to become humble but powerful leaders and servants to the broader community, with a foundational value of radical inclusivity.
- Rockhill Christian Church three hours north of Los Angeles, a church and work program for men and women exiting the prison system, where community members work the farm and often work the steps of ten-step programs and break bread together as a spiritual community.
- New Covenant Church, part of an almost completely White denomination, located in east Oakland, where the White pastor and several White and Asian American members moved into a housing complex to be with the Hmong and Salvadoran and Guatemalan and Vietnamese immigrants, and then found themselves working alongside the community to fight the horrible living conditions created by their slum lord. Developing relationships in the community as equal partners, the face of the congregation and particularly its leadership has diversified significantly over the years.

And that's not including incredibly famous radical and cutting edge churches, such as Glide Memorial Methodist Church in San Francisco, where you are likely to worship between someone off the street and a truly fabulous drag queen on Sunday morning and will be expected to participate

[1]The term "queer" has been intentionally reclaimed by lesbian, gay, bisexual, transgender activists and is often used to be inclusive of all people who identify as "non-heteronormative." It is not intended to be offensive, and in many LGBTQ circles is considered the preferred term.

in the night ministry in the city's roughest neighborhoods or the expansive feeding and shelter programs during the week. That's not including Mission Bay Community Church, the multicultural Presbyterian congregation in San Francisco founded by Bruce Reyes-Chow, providing a spiritually compelling space for second generation API people and mixed-race couples who often struggle to find a space that welcomes their spiritual curiosity and also their complex cultural identity. That's not including the much-talked-about Church for All Saints and Sinners, whose current spiritual struggle is that middle class White people have started attending due to all the attention, and they are trying to figure out how to include them without losing the raw "come as broken as you are" culture they have worked so hard to create.

I also find myself seeing fellow Beloved Community builders in nonprofits:

- Father Greg Boyle's Homeboy Industries in east Los Angeles, where formerly incarcerated gang members develop job skills but also leadership skills and receive the love and hope that allow them to be great fathers and mothers and community members.
- The Grace Lee Boggs Center in Detroit and Detroit Summer, where people who have no government infrastructure are rebuilding Beloved Community in community gardens and in creating meaningful work and living environments that embrace "returned citizens" (their terminology for people released from the prison industrial complex) so that its people can thrive outside of the traditional economic structures that never worked to help them.
- The Delancey Street Foundation in San Francisco and across the country, which founder Mimi Silbert refers to as "the Harvard of the Underclass," where men and women of all races and of warring gang affiliations live together in a community-run home instead of in prison and learn how not to hate each other or

hate themselves as they move toward healing and wholeness personally and within community.

- Restorative justice programs across the entire country, where victims and perpetrators of crimes address the devastation of the crime and find resolution, justice, and healing together.
- The Moral Mondays campaign, through which people of all faiths and races across generations come together every Monday to call on the state legislature in North Carolina to do the right thing by women, immigrants, poor people, African Americans, and the environment. Every week, hundreds and even thousands of people call for a moral approach to legislation that helps all of God's children thrive.
- The East Bay Meditation Center in Oakland, which hosts nights specifically for people with disabilities and chronic pain, for queer people, for people of color, as well as nights for everyone who wants to come. They also do anti-racism work within their leadership and the broader society to build a community responding to systems as well as personal spiritual journeys.

The interesting thing about these congregations and these organizations and movements is they do not treat issues of racial identity or racial and class privilege as luxuries. They learn one another's whole stories and acknowledge where they as individuals and as organizations need to grow to be fully welcoming. They are not communities of good intentions. They are building beloved communities.

To me, Beloved Community is definitely about joy and fullness of being. It's where you and I get to express the complexity of who we are and share the richness of our gifts with one another in ways that benefit the whole community. We've already started engaging in the hard work that makes that vision possible. You see, to me, Beloved Community is also about listening to one another's stories—the beautiful and inspiring parts, but also the painful and even indicting parts—so that we can recognize our personal brokenness and our community's brokenness in order to create healing.

Without that sleeves-rolled-up approach, we only pretend the Beloved Community; we don't actually achieve it.

These groups remind me that Jesus hung out with people on the margins of society and didn't condemn them for not fitting social norms. On a good day, that's what the community of Christ looks like, whether it looks traditional or doesn't look like a church at all.

So I'm hanging out with a pretty random assortment of folks, seeing if we can get the Ubuntu Community off the ground, because, even though such community isn't attached to a particular religion, I can't see Jesus feeling all that at home with a less random assortment. And I am grateful to count you as part of that gloriously random assortment.

May all of us who are building the Beloved Community find each other, support each other, challenge each other to grow and strengthen each other throughout this pre-post-racial era.

"Just when I think Jesus won't survive being deprived of oxygen any longer under the weight of our suffocating indifference to racial intolerance, a prophet like Sandhya Jha steps up. Truthfully, Pre-Post-Racial America is not a book to cozy up next to the fire with. I struggled mightily with each page. That's the point. In afflicting the comfortable and comforting the afflicted, Jha begs us to love our neighbors as ourselves. I pray we listen."

—Jeff Hood, Baptist minister, queer theologian, and prophetic activist

"Wisely using both personal and social narrative Jha's offering gives opportunity for followers of Jesus to practice racial penance in a society that presumes to be post-racial. Jha goes beyond a sterile analysis of race and extends a creative invitation to participate in the Beloved Community."

—Anthony Smith, blogger at Postmodernegro.com